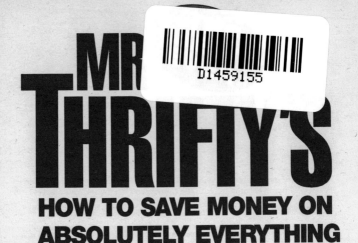

MR THRIFTY'S

HOW TO SAVE MONEY ON ABSOLUTELY EVERYTHING

Third Edition of the Cult Guide
to Smart Living on Less

JANE FURNIVAL

Michael O'Mara Books Limited

First published in Great Britain in 2000

This edition published in Great Britain in 2003 by
Michael O'Mara Books Limited
9 Lion Yard
Tremadoc Road
London SW4 7NQ

A CIP catalogue record for this book is available from the British Library

ISBN 1-84317-056-6

9 10 8

www.mombooks.com

Designed and typeset by Design 23

Printed and Bound by Cox & Wyman Ltd, Reading, Berkshire

To the memory of Sarah, the First Duchess of Marlborough, who saved ink by never dotting her i's.

Jane Furnival lives in Surrey where she looks after her husband, three children, three cats, Boo the huge Bouvier des Flandres dog, rescue hens and vegetable garden. In addition to TV presenting and writing, she runs Jane Furnival's School of Life, which gives short courses on life's finer arts like chocolate-tasting, gift-wrapping and shopping cheaply. Her hobbies are eating chocolate and worrying.

FOR MORE THRIFTY SUGGESTIONS
AND WEBLINKS, SEE

**www.mrthrifty.co.uk and
www.janefurnivalschooloflife.co.uk**

CONTENTS

ACKNOWLEDGEMENTS

Back in 1992, in the depths of a recession, Emma Soames and Richard Ingrams kindly asked me to write a magazine column under the name 'Mr Thrifty'. Then Susan Hill gave Mr Thrifty his golden wings by asking me to write the first book and suggesting the rest of the title, *How To Save Money on Absolutely Everything*. She deserves the credit for its success.

Lesley O'Mara adopted Mr Thrifty and suggested that I write a second edition, and now, this new book. 'Nuff respect, as the homeboys say, for her enthusiasm and commitment and the lunches. Toby Buchan has shepherded it through the presses with tact and quiet assurance.

Ruth Higham has done most of the checking, for which I assume executive responsibility – see the disclaimer at the front of the book. She has also made lots of helpful suggestions, a few ridiculous ones, and that strange tongue-clicking 'dear dear' noise one makes in one's throat whenever I felt fed up, not forgetting the best ideas like, 'Shall I make a cup of tea?'

I am also indebted to everyone who has contributed an idea, including Ms A. Ashbrooke of Powys and Mr Thrifty's fans on various local radio stations around the country who have phoned me on cold Sunday mornings to have a chat. I have tried to name people beside their ideas but apologize if I have left anyone out.

My thanks are always due to my husband Andy Tribble and our children, William, Charlie and Henry for their support and forbearance while I work. Also to Jacqui Bakunowicz and Sara Leyser for helping me in so many ways.

INTRODUCTION

This book will save you more money than you paid for it.

Unless you took it out of the library. Or are standing reading it for free at WHSmith, with all the best cheapskates.

This updated third edition does not replace my two earlier books, but adds to them, and includes more Internet sites and loads of eccentricity, outspokenness, enthusiasm and grumpiness.

I assume that my readers aren't idiots or novices in what are known in certain circles as 'life skills', but are already familiar with basic money-saving habits such as snapping up special offers, and shopping in places like Woolworths, Peacocks and QS, where everyday necessities are cheap. Instead, I hope to reveal new ideas – tricks of the trade, inside secrets and arcane information of the kind that will make you say, 'I didn't know *that*. I must do it.' You won't find this in books that are merely lists of factory shops – though I do direct you to these, where appropriate, in this book.

Thrift is part of the art of living well. Don't confuse it with meanness towards others. It is essentially a private satisfaction, the skill of economizing on boring and invisible necessities like fuel bills, in order to enjoy life's finer things. It is an honourable, aristocratic way of life. Even the Queen has recently given her staff Christmas puddings from Tesco, rather than the more costly Fortnum & Mason variety, *and* used the loyalty points on her bill to gain discounts on other purchases.

If only we heeded her example more. Lavish consumption and show for show's sake is becoming the norm, and it is *so* vulgar, with people boasting of being 'high-maintenance'. But the best, classiest and essentially British way of life is having 'quiet money', being comfortable but not boasting about it. Buy quality goods because they *are* good, not because they have particular labels. If you have inner confidence about who you are, you don't need to impress anyone with a designer name on your T-shirt.

You shouldn't be surprised to learn that millionaires are among Mr Thrifty's most avid fans. I have yet to meet a rich person who is not thrilled to learn new money-saving tips, no matter how trivial. That is often how they became so well off in the first place.

I once met a hard-nosed American stockbroker, who challenged me to find a money-making scheme which he did not already know. As his wife was then pregnant with their first child, I passed on this tip from an old family friend,

Trudy Elliott. Whenever your child is given cash inside a birthday or Christmas card, take half the money and put it into a long-term savings account for them to have when grown up. The stockbroker was delighted with this idea.

Simple notions like this are the essence of thrift. There are basic habits to adopt – such as mending things instead buying new ones, and not going food shopping when hungry – but these days, a truly thrifty person needs extra cunning and caution, because there have been massive changes in the way we think about money and money-saving since *Mr Thrifty* first appeared, in 1994.

The Internet has become an invaluable resource for helping us compare prices, or bagging good deals. But time is also money, especially if you are self-employed. It is wise, these days, to work out an hourly rate for your time. Don't waste it by spending hours on the web or phoning round, trying to shave a few pounds off a bargain price.

Part of the art of thrift is thinking ahead and buying from honest, honourable suppliers at reasonable prices. The idea of real reliability and follow-up service is fast disappearing. Many national companies which offer bargains don't play fair when it comes to replacing faulty products. They hide behind the Internet, or impertinent sales assistants cite 'company policy' as an excuse to drive a coach and horses through the law when they should refund money.

No one can afford to hang onto an unanswered company phone or write letters that are ignored. Shops know this, and it can make them money. In distress, we eventually buy a second computer or kettle and forget the complaint. I call, here and now, for urgent legislation which severely penalizes companies who do not answer letters or complaints promptly and fairly.

Today we are besieged by offers of credit, and it is all too easy to overspend – the average credit card trails £717 debt, according to the latest figures. Nearly half of those who take out credit in shops do it on the spur of the moment. And a recent survey of teenagers revealed that most of them thought that the biggest living expenditure, when setting up their own home, would be on clothes and going out.

If you or someone you know is struggling, I should avoid private debt management services, some of whose methods are dubious and expensive. Many companies will agree to freeze your debt and take payments at a lower, affordable rate. Or for free, confidential advice, ask the Citizens Advice Bureau. Alternatively, talk to the National Debtline, 0808 808 4000, or the Consumer Credit Counselling Service, 0800 138 1111. Also, everyone might be wise to get a

Budget Planner and the leaflets *Top Ten Credit Tips* and *Think Before You Borrow* from the Office of Fair Trading, www.oft.gov.uk or OFT, PO Box 366, Hayes, Middlesex UB3 1XB, 0870 606 0321.

• **To get a good overview of your finances, use the Motley Fool 'state of affairs calculator' at www.fool.co.uk/debt/articles/soacalc.htm**

HOW TO SAVE MONEY ON ANYTHING AND EVERYTHING

Pay cash

The question, 'Can you offer me money off this, if I pay cash?' works wonders, especially if you produce the cash, discreetly, as you speak. Even if you only have two £10 notes and intend to come back later with the rest, the sight of ready money has a magical effect. The shop is delighted to save the 3% cost of processing cheques or waiting for credit card payments to come through. Don't waste time negotiating with junior shop assistants: always ask for the manager or a senior salesperson.

Don't look or act as if you are well off

If you dress smartly, shopkeepers assume you can afford to pay top price. This is the secret of many antiquarian book buyers when haggling for masterpieces in shops.

Ask for a discount – and give the shop a reason to say 'yes'

If you can spot a dent, a scratch, or any superficial damage at all, offer to take the item as seen, from the display. Don't appear *too* keen to buy, and act *most* concerned when you first spot the damage, pointing out the inconvenience to you. A missing button, though easy enough to replace, can be worth up to 25% off. Ripped packaging can also get a discount if you explain that it is for a present and you will have to rewrap it. I once netted 40% off the price of an armchair by making a fuss about a slight hair gel stain left on the headrest.

Start a friendly relationship with the seller by looking him or her in the eye and giving them a face-saving reason to give you a discount. Are you buying more than one thing from the shop? Are you a regular customer? Is it the last one in a hard-to-sell size or colour? Can you take it away there and then, or collect it yourself, saving delivery? If you are having curtains made, have you bought the fabric at the shop?

Ask, 'What's your best price for this?'
Smile as you say it. The phrase is worth its weight in gold.

Walk away
Don't be haughty, but say, 'It's wonderful, but not *that* wonderful' and leave. When you come back later, the dealer may have softened. After an initially unsuccessful negotiation, I once had a man run into the street after me with a pair of slippers wrapped up in a bag and say, 'Here they

are. I didn't want anyone else to see me give you the discount.'

Go back an hour before closing time
This works well in craft and country fairs and shows, but also in supermarkets and even on the last day of the Harrods sale. Sellers don't want to reload stock into their vans.

Throw in a bottle of wine
My garage always collects and drops my car round to me, although that is not their normal service. They know that I always give the driver a bottle of wine.

Buy in bulk
You can usually negotiate good deals especially with mail-order firms. I buy a whole lamb from a friendly farm each spring. It arrives in all its cuts, ready for the freezer. Commercial cleaning solutions are also cheaper direct from the commercial retailers than in supermarkets, as they are sold by the gallon. Transfer into smaller garden spray bottles.

Be an old lady, or be friendly with one

Old ladies rule the earth when it comes to getting
things for nothing. Keep a tough but frail-looking
lady to 'front' any negotiations you have,
especially with workmen. It is a myth that they
rip old people off: many charge a minimal fee or
even do things for free. A friend of mine actually
got her £40 parking ticket cancelled by the
manager of a branch of Sainsbury's by pointing
out that she was an OAP. She shooed me away,
saying she needed to do her 'vulnerable old lady
act'. Old people also receive discounts on certain
days in many shops. Wyevale Garden Centres has
a 10% off card for those over 60 (0800 413 213,
www.wyevale.co.uk) as do Focus DIY superstores
(01270 501555, www.focusdiy.co.uk). If they buy
things on your behalf, offer to split the saving
you have made with them as their commission.

Shop in cheap areas of town

Many national shop chains, from supermarkets to
dry-cleaners, charge cheaper prices for identical
goods and services in poorer areas. This makes
doing a big food shop in a poorer area worth the
accumulated saving. Under 'poorer areas' I
include most ordinary old-fashioned high streets;
the heart of Britain being ripped out by silly
traffic systems discouraging cars, by high rents,
and by the rise of glamorous out-of-town malls
with free parking. However, you will find better
bargains in charity shops and jumble sales in

more affluent areas: rich people tend to throw out nicer things.

Other advantages of poor areas are 'grey shops' which import overstocks from other parts of the world, so you might find Persil with Arabic writing on the box at a cheaper price, for example. Similar are 'pound shops' – called all sorts of names in which the word 'pound' usually figures. Here, most things cost £1 for three – from candles to Camembert.

Ethnic shops generally offer great savings if you buy rice by the sack or olive oil by the gallon.

On weekdays, tour the wholesale areas of cities, like Cheetham Hill in Manchester, or the Spitalfields area in London. Shoes, electronics, clothes – few wholesalers will refuse to sell you something, especially for cash.

Cash and carry shops
These are the places which supply corner shops with huge quantities of anything you can name. You will need to add VAT to the price labels. To gain entry, you usually need to apply in advance, or be introduced by a member, and may need a business card or VAT number. Ask around.

MAKRO has thirty branches nationwide selling food and drink by the case, computers – their own brand or whatever comes in – garden equipment and hardware. You need to register in advance before shopping. You (or a friend you can go in with) must be a 'caterer, trader, or professional business user' which means in practice VAT-registered, or self-employed; or you may qualify if you have responsibility for ordering things for a business and can show two invoices addressed to you from suppliers or your name as a director on company headed paper. I know someone who successfully showed a letter from a company director explaining that she was buying for a company party.

• **Application hotline, 0800 450 0000; headquarters 0161 707 3757, www.makro.co.uk**

Save time and effort in a one-stop shop

Many bargain hunters never think of John Lewis, who deliver nationally. The store prices routinely match the lowest found in local shops, so you save time hunting around. The staff are more informed and impartial than most, so they can normally give reasonable advice. Their promise, 'Never knowingly undersold', means that they will refund the difference if you find an item you have bought from them sold at a lower price anywhere in Britain. They consider claims made within twenty-eight days of your purchase, as long as you are comparing exactly the same item, including colour, and the price quoted elsewhere is not a special price for particular people, for example, storecard holders. They also exclude items from market stalls, duty-free shops, mail order catalogues or the Internet, as they say they can't check the goods and the standards of service and support are lower. Although prices for their Internet service are identical to those in the shops, check the delivery charge before you buy via the website. Ordering by telephoning the store may save money, as delivery is sometimes free within a certain radius, whereas the website always charges.

• **Headquarters: John Lewis, Oxford St, London W1A 1EX, 020 7629 7711, www.johnlewis.com**

Getting 10% off anything

Index (0845 755 2211) and Argos (0870 600 1010) are reliably cheap for catalogue shopping and stores. Traditional mail order catalogues, like Littlewoods and Freemans, also offer long credit and house, car and medical insurance in instalments. You can also get 10% back on orders from these traditional catalogues if you first sign up to be an agent. You have to place orders worth over £100, not just from yourself but from others. Then you get back £1 for every £10 in orders, or goods valued £1.25.

• **Littlewoods have the same number as Index, 0845 755 2211, www.littlewoods.co.uk**

• Freemans, 0800 731 9731, www.freemans.com

• www.kaysnet.com (0870 151 0541) offers 10% off your first purchase of anything

Cashback
www.greasypalm.co.uk sends you a rebate cheque when you shop through the site with a range of high street shops.

Perks from storecards
If you are thinking about a major purchase, call the shop and ask if they are going to have a storecard promotion. This means that if you apply for a storecard on a particular day, you receive 10% off purchases made on the first day, or some similar incentive. If you already have a storecard, your partner or friend can apply for one and secure the discount for you.

Storecard holders usually get 10% off sale prices and a preview day to snap up the best bargains. My Harvey Nichols card gives me cheap parking at the car park in Harriet Street behind the store, but if you don't have a card, show a bill for the minimum sum stipulated at the entrance to get the parking discount.

• Harvey Nichols, 109-125 Knightsbridge, London SW1X 7RJ, 020 7235 5000, www.harveynichols.com

Use a personal shopper and get a free glass of wine

Most department stores and some hotels have a free personal shopping service. This saves time and is very luxurious, even if you only want an egg timer. You make an appointment and are greeted in a sumptuous private suite, with tea, cold drinks and snacks laid on free. You are given the opportunity to try things on in privacy and luxury, with a glass of wine to hand.

There are also freelance personal shoppers all over the country, who charge an hourly or daily rate to take you on a planned expedition and may be able to negotiate a discount with the shops, or know cheap places, saving you enough to justify their fee. Normally, but not always, these shoppers concentrate on clothes – from wedding to fancy dress – and charge from £35 an hour.

• Try www.imagecounts.co.uk or contact Jenny, 020 7407 6764, or see local experts listed in the Yellow Pages

'Do anything services'

For people who are cash rich but time poor, a 'concierge' or 'personal assistant service' like Ten.uk claims to save you an average of a hundred hours a year by trouble-shooting and problem-solving without limit. They will find reliable workmen, book a holiday, upgrade a flight, secure impossible restaurant bookings and wait in at your home for deliveries, using a workforce of security-vetted former military guards on scooters. A basic service costs between £50 and £75 per month depending on how often you use it; the VIP service, in which they manage everything on a project from start to finish, costs £150 monthly, and they don't charge extra unless they have to leave the office. 0700 010 1999, www.tenuk.co.uk for more details.

• **Also try Entrust, £400 monthly, in London and the South-East, Manchester and Leeds, 0870 908 8008, www.entrust-net.com**

I have also seen these kind of services offered free by credit card companies, but whenever I have used them, they have been of little use, for example, the hotel-booking service which returned to me days later, when all available rooms I wanted had been booked up, saying it could only book rooms in certain large hotel groups and could not suggest other places.

Cheaper personal help

I always ask my best local school whether they have any helpful sixth-formers available. They come, under the watchful eye of mum, to cut the grass and move heavy furniture and can be of great assistance. Also try asking foreign language students from local colleges or students from catering colleges.

Buy a farm, a car or anything big at auction

Buying at auction is the cheapest way to buy anything. I don't know why the TV programme *Bargain Hunt* buys at fairs and sells at auctions when dealers, who make their livings from it, do exactly the reverse.

Auction News is a monthly magazine carrying details of every sale to be carried out by Official Receivers, county courts, the Ministry of Defence and the police. Brave the closed-shop atmosphere and you can buy everything from houses, cattle and land to computers and cars at a fraction of the price you would normally pay – for instance a £380 washing machine for £75.

Mr Thrifty readers can save over £20 on an annual subscription, paying £39.50 instead of £50. Quote 'Mr Thrifty offer', Code 1005, Wentworth Publishing, 17 Fleet Street, London EC4Y 1AA, 020 7353 7300.

If you are impatient, short-notice sales are listed on a dial-a-fax hotline. Call and press your fax machine's 'receive' button for a list. 60p per minute. 0906 602 1558

• **Also try Frank G. Bowen, 73 Sceptre Road, London E2 OJU, 020 7790 7272 for bankrupt stock, from clothes to computers**

• **01332 551300, www.auctionnews.co.uk**

Lost property auctions

London Transport sells thousands of unclaimed items at twenty-six sales a year at Greasby's auctioneers in Tooting, South London. 'Mundane' items like gloves, wallets, bibles and pushchairs are grouped into bundles of twenty. 'Value' things like Rolexes and musical instruments go into a more select auction but still sell for bargain prices, for example, an £800 camcorder for £250. They are far from being glamorous occasions, however, and there is a small charge for attending the auctions.

• Greasby's, 211 Longley Road, Tooting, London SW17 9LG
020 8672 2972

Car boot sales

Local papers and *Exchange & Mart* list sales where local people and small traders sell junk, toys, clothes, motor spares and antiques. Newark in Nottinghamshire is considered the best antiques fair in Britain.

• Also try www.carbootcalendar.com, 01981 251 633
• www.carbootjunction.com, 07793 749 650
• www.sellingthings.net/collect/car-boot-sales

A guide to discount shops

The Good Deal Directory lists all Britain's bargain shops, factory outlets, discount warehouses and shopping villages. It also pays £10 for new recommendations, so you can save the money paid for a copy. £9.99 plus £1.50 p&p, PO Box 4, Lechlade, Glos GL7 3YB. 01367 86 0016, www.gooddealdirectory.co.uk

Savings, both silly and sensible

The Tightwad Gazette flourished for over six years in America. No saving was too trivial for devotees to mention. It lives on in book form as *The Complete Tightwad Gazette: Promoting Thrift as a Viable Alternative Lifestyle*, Issues I, II, III and 'The Last Issues', by Amy Dacyczyn. Available from www.amazon.com 0800 279 6630, from $13.99 plus p&p, but you can pick up a second-hand copy from $13.25 from the same source.

• For a free currency converter enabling you to check foreign prices before buying on the Net, see www.xe.com

• Also check www.cheapskatemonthly.com for Mary Hunt's constantly updated tips

A really useful directory

Alison Cork's 'Really Useful' column in the London *Evening Standard* is full of interesting tips about services and discounts, but she has also gathered lots of recommendations together in a directory, which is London-biased, though not exclusively so. £4.95 including p&p from The Really Useful Directory, PO Box 38248, London NW3 1XE, 020 7431 7909, email info@rudirect.com

Claim reward points carefully

Naturally you will be a member of any rewards or points scheme offered by shops and petrol stations. It pays to be aware of their various deals. Goldfish, for instance, gives back a princely 75p per £100 spent. But spend it wisely! Normally to get £10 off your British Gas bill, you need 1500 points. But you only need 1250 points for £10 off your purchases at Marks & Spencer, Dixons, Homebase or TV licence vouchers.

Saving by shopping online

Online traders can sell more cheaply as they have no shop to run and maintain. The downside is that some can take a long time to send your goods because they stockpile orders until they have enough to secure a big discount from the makers. E-traders can also be slippery when goods break down, or need returning. Some things to remember when buying online are:

– Protect yourself by dealing only with UK-based Internet retailers. Companies based abroad can slap on massive unexpected delivery and tax charges, some don't answer your messages, and they are not bound by our consumer laws when anything goes wrong – a problem which the Office of Fair Trading is addressing by trying to hold the credit card companies responsible for purchases made abroad. My personal feeling is that you might as well try to tie a python in a bow, but good luck to them! Check that the site has an address and phone number, and phone them up. Surprisingly, some big Internet dealers don't list phone numbers so you can't contact them in a crisis.

– Safeguard yourself by checking if the Internet trader is a member of TrustUK, a government-endorsed trade organization which also deals with complaints. www.trustuk.org.uk

– If you want to buy something from abroad, especially from America, you may save money by finding a friend out there to buy it on your behalf and send it to you as a gift. If you send them something from here there is no need to pay the extra tax sometimes demanded. If you want to buy securely, and you don't want to give out your credit card number, investigate Splash Plastic. This works like a pay-as-you-go mobile phone card, but with money. Buy a card via the website www.splashplastic.com which you charge up with cash at a newsagent. If you lose the card, you have only lost the value you have charged it with and no more. Retailers that accept Splash Plastic at the moment are limited but more will come on board. CD Wow, www.countrybookshop.co.uk, and www.bloomsbury.com will take Splash.

– Check the websites of your favourite shops and sign up for online newsletters. Most companies use these sites to dispose of end-of-line bargains, which you won't see in the shops. www.allshopsuk.co.uk/shops/offers.htm has a page of current offers and deals available online.

– www.letsbuyit.com offers bargains on electronics, for instance, a home theatre system reduced from £300 to £120. You have to become a partner – which is free – and sign up for the deal. If enough people sign up, it secures a discount for bulk ordering from the manufacturer. It is quite thorough about what you do if you want to cancel an order or return a product – basically, you then deal direct with the selling partner/agent.

– www.pricerunner.com (020 7839 8382) offers independent price comparisons and expert information for various categories including cars, computers and power bills.

– www.ebay.com or www.ebay.co.uk is an auction site enabling you to sell and buy anything second-hand. Potential buyers bid for advertised items; it is up to the seller to accept their offer and deal with them personally. The buyer pays p&p costs.

– www.loot.com has 140,000 advertisements for second-hand items online.

– Several sites compare prices, without selling anything directly, but check delivery costs before deciding to buy. Try www.dealtime.co.uk

www.abcaz.com www.kelkoo.co.uk
www.pricerunner.co.uk www.simplesaver.co.uk
rounds up all the companies offering discounts
and bargains that week – both shops and by
Internet – you can only browse around what is
there, not specify what you want to buy. Also try:
www.ciao.co.uk www.empiredirect.co.uk for hi-
fis, TV, electronics and www.abargain.co.uk for
bikes.

• For the latest discount vouchers, try www.vouchervault.co.uk,
www.greedymoose.co.uk, www.instantcouponz.com and
www.offersandfreebies.co.uk

Advice on what's most reliable
£75 gives you an annual subscription to *Which?*,
the Consumers Association magazine, providing
rigorous buyers' reports on anything you can
name. You get four complimentary back issues of
your choice when you subscribe.

• 0800 252 100, www.which.co.uk

Personal recommendations
The Good Housekeeping Institute offers excellent
consumer reports in the main *Good Housekeeping*
magazine, and a separate magazine called *GHI
Choice*. On Fridays between 11am and 5pm, there is
a personal phone line offering specific answers to
individual queries costing 75p per minute.

• For household goods, call 0906 752 9070; for food and cooking queries, 0906 752 9080. Also try www.ivillage.com

Freebies

– Plastic gloves and paper towels are free next to petrol station pumps.

– Sugar, salt, sauce sachets, etc. are available from most cafes. I use the sugar bags in water for my cut flowers, to make them last longer.

– Sweets and lollipops. Many shops, cafes, hairdressers and even antique dealers, keep sweets on the counter. Popping in on some made-up errand, then asking 'Can I have some for my little boy?' usually garners a good selection. Unless the shop is actually selling sweets!

– Matches. From bars, hotels, hairdressers and restaurants.

– Postcards. Usually found in places like coffee shops, trendy bookshops and Odeon cinemas.

– Rubber bands. The postman drops these outside front doors. Look around wherever anyone you know receives lots of post.

– Wrapping paper. Florists give away nice sheets whenever you buy flowers. If you want to buy more, ask whether they will sell a whole roll, or whether they will buy one for you or take you with them when they next go to the wholesaler. Florists' wrap is gigantic, much larger than a roll of wallpaper, will last all year and costs only a few pounds.

– Newspapers and sometimes magazines. Read free on the Internet or at the local library or cafe, although you have to buy a drink at the latter.

– Finding useful junk thrown away in the streets. Skip-trawling is not what it was, although you might still tour rich areas, factories and shops, and even fruit shops and florists, just after they close. Fine bits of wood used in floors are useful as kindling wood, as long as they haven't been painted or treated. It is illegal to take anything from a skip without the owner's permission, a rule that should be obeyed by all.

– www.freebieholics.co.uk reports on the latest free offers across the Internet. Also try www.thefreesite.com, www.freestuffjunction.co.uk, www.free-uk-shares.co.uk or www.freeukstuff.net

– www.couponmountain.co.uk tips you off about current discount offers and those companies offering free postage and packing.

– Many companies offer freebies in exchange for friends' details. See www.referralfreebies.co.uk

– The BBC offers freebies if you go onto their website www.bbc.co.uk/radio1/onelife/fun/freebies.shtml

Go and live in Scotland
Where you are either too remote from shops to bother to buy much, and anyway, you are so punch-drunk on the natural beauty of the area, you don't want much; or the shops in the towns are incredibly cheap.

Where there is a culture of saving money. Shop assistants will beg you not to buy something too expensive, but suggest something else. They can't stop themselves: it is in their national nature.

Where, if you are a student, the government pays your university fees. If elderly or infirm, it pays your care home bill.

HOW TO SAVE THOUSANDS ON BUYING A HOUSE

These days savings and investments produce such a poor return, and are taxed so unfairly, that it is worth considering whether to stop paying into a pension scheme and use the money to pay a mortgage on a house instead. If you already have one home, think about buy-to-let homes or a country place – property should keep its value.

• **www.homeowner.loanspage.co.uk will search for good interest deals for you.**

Build it yourself

Building skills can be easy to master, or you can buy a plot of land and get a builder to do the work while you supervise.

As a useful introduction and debunker of myths, *The Housebuilder's Bible* is a miracle guide to doing any work on a house, written in an easy, funny and practical style. Author Mark Brinkley covers niggles such as, 'Is that tree too close to my house?' with a helpful table specifying each tree type and its correct distance from your supporting walls. His chapter on 'How to double your building costs' points out that style costs money. An ordinary fireplace may cost £250; an inglenook, £4000, and handmade floor and wall tiles add over two thousand pounds to the average cost.

• £18 including p&p from Ovolo Publishing, Orchard House, Heath Road, Warboys, Cambridgeshire PE28 2UW, 01487 824704, www.rodelia.co.uk

Save thousands on home improvements

The Self Build and Home Improvement Centre chain, operated by BuildStore, has a variety of ways to save money, even if you want to rewire a plug rather than build your own home.

The free Selfbuild Materials Trade Account card saves you around 10% on everything from building materials to electrical supplies, including home appliances, kitchens, bathrooms and floor coverings bought at various stores around the country. The biggest chain which accepts it is Jewson – who give card holders a lower discount than you would get if you approached them as a one-off self-builder and also boast a special 'account manager' who will advise how to save money if you consult him before you buy anything. HSS, which hires out equipment from floor sanders to scaffolding and even bouncy castles for children's parties, gives Selfbuild card holders 25% off hire prices in the brochure – more than the 10% discount they offer their own cardholders. The card can also act as a credit card for materials with a limit of between £15,000 and £25,000. 0800 870 9497 for applications.

The 'plotsearch' service on the BuildStore website lists all available plots in Britain, together with aerial photographs to save time and petrol inspecting the site. The company offers self-build mortgages in which tranches of cash are paid at the start of each stage of the build, not at the end of it, as is more usual, so you can negotiate better prices for cash payment for materials and labour. There is a two-year building site insurance scheme which converts to free building insurance cover at the end of your build. Most self-build insurance only covers you while the build is happening – usually for a period of eighteen months.

• 0870 870 9991, www.buildstore.co.uk

How to get hold of good workmen

From Penny Butler, a mother of three who built her own house, comes this tip. The Association of Self Builders is a non-profit-making club for anyone renovating, converting, extending or building a house. £30 annual membership gives you local contacts, ideas and good workmen, bulletins, information sheets and a video library. Members also get insurance discounts and massive discounts on building materials at Jewsons and Graham. To join, go to www.self-builder.co.uk.

Buy an abandoned or derelict property at half its market value

Friends of mine went hunting for a small cottage near London and ended up buying a boarded-up mansion in Shropshire. The experience changed their lives and they now operate a very superior bed and breakfast called Old Colehurst Manor, where a stay includes ghosts free of charge. If you fall in love with a wreck – I mean a building, not a person – and can stand living in a caravan in the garden while it is done up, Estate Track specializes in locating owners of abandoned and derelict property. The £50 fee gives you a standard search seeking the owner for the last forty years. For £250, they can trace the last living relatives of the property's registered owner. In their experience, these relatives have no idea that they owned this property and usually sell at between 40% to 50% of its market value.

• Estate Track, 0800 083 2194, www.propertysearch.com

Do up a wreck

Another advantage of buying derelict houses is that you avoid stamp duty, the house-buying tax which kicks in at £600 when you buy a home worth £60,000. Ask your local authority planning department for a look at the Buildings At Risk register.

Alternatively, ask your local authority if it runs a

Homesteading scheme. This offers council-owned houses in need of repair, at about a third off the market price.

• **The charity Save Britain's Heritage tries to save falling-down historical buildings from cottages to warehouses. Most are listed and unoccupied, and not on any estate agent's books, although the owners may be open to offers. The annual catalogue costs £10, including p&p, and lists about a hundred buildings. You can see the complete register for £15 on the Internet at www.savebritainsheritage.org where you can also find a free sample. Save Britain's Heritage, 70 Cowcross Street, London EC1M 6EJ, 020 7253 3500**

• **The Society for the Protection of Ancient Buildings, SPAB, also has a list. 020 7377 1644, www.spab.org.uk**

• **Capital Property Lists also has a list of homes in need of TLC. It costs £25 to receive lists each two months. 020 7288 0288, www.capital-property.com**

Buy a repossessed house

Repossessed and derelict houses are sold for a fraction of their true value. While there is no free central list, you can buy one from private companies like www.numberone4property.co.uk and www.repossessedhousesforsale.co.uk.

It is also worth asking your local authority and estate agents. They tend to keep repossessions under the counter as their low prices depress local ordinary house prices. Before making an offer, check a property's market value free at www.ourproperty.co.uk which is based on Land Registry prices.

Buying a home at auction

Auctions are listed in local papers; you might also find that estate agents will be able to help. You must brave a closed circle of property developers who view things together and buy whole blocks of homes. Also ask for a free 'infopack' as they call it, from Property Auction News, 01709 365911.

Where to find the cheapest flats

Flats over shops tend to be the cheapest option. If you buy one to do up, check the generous tax allowances on the cost of refurbishment. I suggest not buying a flat over a fast-food shop: there are fire risks that make it harder to get a mortgage on. Of course, you could then buy the fast-food shop and call it the kitchen...

Unusual country homes at realistic prices

In the Sticks magazine lists distinctive country homes like converted cattle sheds and chapels, and offers information on architecture, culture and travel in the areas covered. £38 for twelve issues. 01434 382680, www.inthesticks.com.

Housing Associations

Housing Associations have a variety of offers called things like 'shared ownership', 'equity loan schemes' and 'key worker options' to bring down the price of homes for first-time buyers and key workers (those workers involved in keeping essential services running, such as teachers, policemen and women, 999 service workers, junior doctors and nurses). Your local council should have more information on local housing associations. You must ring to get onto the 'official register' before becoming eligible for a housing association home. Also contact your local authority for new schemes. Several councils have properties earmarked for key workers. Search the internet by putting the words 'keyworkers' and your town name into a search engine. Also try www.keyworkers.org, 020 8371 5066.

House swopping

If you can't sell your house, don't want to be stuck in a chain or want to cut your mortgage by moving to a smaller place, you can try exchanging homes. You save estate agents' fees, pay little or no deposit and no stamp duty if you receive under £60,000 in top-up fees to make the exchange equal.

Get your home valued (free) by several estate agents, take the average price and put a photo and details in the local paper and newsagent windows of the area you want to move to, stating what you seek in return.

If you want to move to a more expensive new home, most builders will take your home in part exchange. Barratts, for instance, have new and old homes for sale around the country. You must trade up 30% and pay a reservation fee. Call 0151 357 4800 for details. Check the property section of any newspaper for other offers.

Avoiding paying stamp duty

Stamp duty, the government tax payable when buying a home, costs 1% on houses between £60,000 and £250,000, 3% on homes up to £500,000 and 4% after that. If your home has a value bordering on that sum, take into account the fixtures and fittings and ask for a separate price for them, which does not attract stamp duty. Be honest about this, though: checks are made.

• **The government has scrapped stamp duty in 'disadvantaged' areas – for a list of these, see www.inlandrevenue.gov.uk You will need to know the property's postcode. For this, ask at a post office or call 08457 111222 or look it up at www.royalmail.co.uk/quicktools/postcode**

Save on estate agents' fees

Never pay the first fee the estate agent quotes: play them off against each other and bargain with them. Remember that they charge VAT on top of the fee. If you don't mind haggling with potential buyers and personally showing them round your home, consider advertising your home yourself.

Link-Up Properties charges flat-rate commission on houses it sells plus £95 registration fee for six months' marketing, including advertising in national papers and online. The price – which you don't pay if they fail to find you a buyer in eight weeks – is £250 including VAT for homes under £100,000 and £500 for homes over that. They thriftily point out that you can save £250 on a borderline valued property by putting it on at £99,999. They don't come and value your home, and you write your own description, buy their 'for sale' board (£23.50) and put it up yourself. 0800 072 0800, www.linkprop.co.uk.

• Also look at www.halfapercent.com, which operates only within the M25, 0871 424 0424; www.fish4homes.co.uk www.assertahomes.com www.rightmove.co.uk

Get fixed price conveyancing

Make sure that you get a quote for a fixed fee from your solicitor, otherwise the sky can be the limit. There is no need to use a local practitioner for conveyancing as any solicitor in any part of the country can do it. £164.50 excluding petty expenses (maximum £35), disbursements, fees for money transmission, professional indemnity and work done for a lender is a typical quote from Nigel Broadhead, Mynard Solicitors (NAT 1), 0845 741 9461.

Save bother before buying

Surveys and solicitors' searches only go so far. www.upmystreet.com gives detailed information about a neighbourhood before you move into it – from removals companies and cleaners to the best-performing schools, crime rates and all sorts of information including past property values. I know someone who used it during a court case with his ex-wife, in which he proved that she sold her home for considerably more than she claimed.

www.homecheck.co.uk 0870 606 1700, collates information about environmental hazards like air pollution, subsidence and whether a house is near a landfill site and therefore likely to have problems with gas or chemical pollution. The service is free: for a detailed 'Homecheck Professional' report, you pay £29 plus VAT.

Save 10% on DIY and garden items

DIY superstores Focus offer a 10% off Advantage card for the first six months, for those who have just moved house, www.focusdiy.co.uk 01270 501555.

How to get 20% off building materials

Find a builders' merchant (Yellow Pages will help). Go in once to show your face and make a small purchase, like nails. Return for something else and ask for your 'trade loyalty' discount. You won't be asked to prove that you're a builder since, frankly, many workmen don't have a card and the shop wants to shift its stock.

Using workmen

Things to bear in mind when you have workmen in your house are:

– Do not expect them to look after your things. Your home is a 'site' to them. Never leave them to cover your things up and remove anything of value to safety.

– Never go out and leave them alone, especially to finish off. Similarly, never leave them to lock up; ask a neighbour to do it.

– Pay them only when they have finished, and check that they have painted even hidden areas, like skirting boards, corners, and door edges.

– You will find it easy to negotiate discounts for cash. I sometimes throw in a bottle of wine which tends to produce better prices the next time they come.

– I have found it easier to employ workmen through a small building firm rather than as one-off tradespeople. Then there is an intermediary who will tell them to tidy up, not to smoke in your home, etc.

Get a warranty on building work

Most trade organizations exist to protect their members who pay their dues, rather than the public and, although they have complaints procedures, they are often not worth pursuing. For a cast-iron guarantee on major building work get a warranty from a member of the Federation of Master Builders, 020 7242 7583, www.findabuilder.co.uk. That protects against the risk of the builder leaving the job unfinished and vouchsafes the work for the next two years. Your builder member must apply before starting the job and you pay 1% of the contract price. Other insurance-backed guarantees come from the National Register of Warranted Builders, 020 7404 4155.

Always tell your insurers before you have major work done, otherwise, if you, the house or the builder is damaged, they may not allow the claim.

Plumbing repairs

Resist having a water meter installed close to your home. Your water board is responsible for pipe repairs up to the meter; from there, it is down to you if you get an underground leak or burst pipe. A blocked drain costs on average £125; a burst main, £205. Water boards also offer an emergency repair service like Thames Water's Home Service at £52.95 a year. You get a workperson within two hours, up to £2,000 per claim to unblock and replace external pipes and up to £1,000 to repair plumbing inside your home, with no bill to pay up front. 0800 783 3344.

Clear blocked sinks and lavatories with a wire coathanger unpicked and poked down the U-bend. Or try an old-fashioned mop, which works like a plunger when pumped up and down – all plumbers carry one. Before calling a plumber, buy caustic soda from a hardware shop to burn the blockage; or an insider's tip is One-Stop Drain Cleaner found in most hardware shops.

If you are not sure how to turn off your water in an emergency, or can't operate stiff brass valves, buy a SureStop switch, which can even be operated by remote control. £29.95, 0121 782 5666.

Decorating at a discount
Always buy Dulux trade paint or any other trade paint, rather than ordinary paint. Obtainable from builders' merchants, it is cheaper, goes further and is easier to apply.

Check wallpaper and fabrics outside the shop before buying, or take a sample home. The light will make it look completely different. Always ask for a discount when buying large amounts.

• **Just Fabrics, 01566 776279, www.justfab.co.uk, has one of the largest sample stocks in the country and offers many items at a discount**

There are a variety of suppliers of curtain fabric offering substantial discounts on curtain fabric from top manufacturers. It is worth calling a few of these and comparing prices, but before starting, make sure that you know the fabric and colour number, found on the back of samples in sample books. Try Top Service, 0160 868 4829; Designer Fabrics, 0127 061 0032; Discount Designer Fabrics 0870 241 2527, www.discount-designer-fabrics.com Fabrics and Wallpapers 0800 018 8470, www.designercloth.co.uk

• **www.wallpaperdirect.co.uk will send free samples of all top makes, help you calculate how many rolls you need and provide you with lots of tips**

My grandmother made her own shampoo from eggs and beer, and the thrifty will be delighted to learn that it can double as paint, with the right additions. See *The Natural Paint Book* by Lynn Edwards and Julia Lawless, £16.99, Kyle Cathie, available from bookshops or www.amazon.co.uk.

Second-hand curtains
The Curtain Exchange takes good quality cast-offs and sells them, normally only if lined, at 50% to 60% of their value. If buying you can take curtains home for a 24-hour test first. www.thecurtainexchange.net 01376 561199.

You can buy discount blinds from www.blinds2go.co.uk

Cheap curtain material

I use old tablecloths, either from ancient family stocks at the bottom of chests of drawers, or just buy them from a cheap shop or charity shop. Crisp white embroidered linen tablecloths look smart as window blinds and need no hemming.

• **TOFFS, The Old-Fashioned Fabric Shop, sells lots of cheap, serviceable fabrics you may have thought you would never see again. You can find ticking for pillow-making, canvas for deckchair covers, as well as calico and hessian for the base of your sofa. 020 8778 8049**

• **A free booklet called *Learn to Love Stoddard* gives carpet buyers all the information they could crave about carpet care and cleaning. 0800 027 4888, www.stoddardcarpets.com**

Where to revamp a kitchen for under £50 and buy cheap hardware

Screwfix, the catalogue used by professional builders, sells everything including the kitchen sink at trade prices, and also provides a next-day delivery service (excluding Sundays) for a small charge, or even for free, depending on your order. My favourite bargain is a replacement pine kitchen door at £2.75. You can order Slim Save heaters, which are very thin, and which cost 3p an hour to use, as well as longlife light bulbs. You can also pick up those emergency exit signs with running men on them – the perfect present for a blushing groom on his stag night!

Before ordering, read the blurb about prices and delivery because it explains a complex system of extra discounts: but basically, the more you spend, the more discount you rack up, to £100 off £1000. There are also bulk order discounts. The order line is open till 10pm during the week and till 8pm on weekends and bank holidays. There is also a clearance warehouse at Mead Avenue, Houndstone Business Park, Yeovil.

• **Screwfix Direct, Freepost, Yeovil BA22 8BF. 0500 41 41 41, www.screwfix.com**

Pay less for home improvements by buying from France

The three big French DIY chains are Leroy Merlin, 00 33 321 965 050, www.leroymerlin.com Mr Bricolage, 00 33 321 303 630, www.mr-bricolage.fr and Castorama, 00 33 321 972 500, www.castorama.fr
A recent Eurotunnel survey demonstrated that you can make big savings by buying in France. Everything from taps to rugs and curtain rails were half UK prices, with beech flooring 31% cheaper. Before buying fittings like taps, check sizes – although with today's metric standards, these should be identical. If the goods are faulty, a new EU sales directive gives buyers the right to take them back if they do not 'conform to contract', as long as this is done within 'a reasonable time'.

• **For more information, check www.day-tripper.net**

Cheap appliances

Take your common sense with you when shopping for appliances. It is hundreds of pounds cheaper to buy an ordinary fridge and put it inside a cupboard than to buy a built-in one. 'Integrated' machines have the disadvantage of having their controls situated inside the door, so you can't check on the progress of your dishwasher without opening the door and getting splashed.

Be wary of using kitchen companies who are tied into specific appliance-suppliers. When the machine goes wrong, you have to ask the kitchen company to get the repairer, and in many cases, once they have your money, they are neglectful of the aftersales service.

• www.cheap-washing-machines.co.uk links to sites offering top brand models including AEG, Baumatic, Bosch, Candy, Hotpoint, Whirlpool and Miele, at heavily discounted prices

• www.trade-appliances.co.uk sells over 3,000 appliances at around 40% off and also has special offers

• www.unbeatable.co.uk offers huge discounts off appliances and electronics. 01293 543555

• Buyers and Sellers (020 7229 1947) or Hot and Cold Inc (020 8960 1200) are also worth asking. The latter have been known to give an appliance a swift kick and say: 'It's damaged so you can have money off.'

Hiring home appliances

DER Direct (0870 010 2238) and Box Clever (0870 010 0115) offer home appliances to rent, from TVs to washing machines, from £3.46 a month including all servicing. If you live in a shared house or can't afford to buy a machine, try the money-in-the-slot option. They fix a sum and take it from the machine as rent. The rest of the money in the machine is given back to you.

Should you buy a service contract or warranty with an appliance?

No. You are already protected by consumer laws. Enlightened sellers, such as Asda, offer a free three-year warranty on all TVs, videos and DVDs, and have said that they believe expensive extended warranties are simply a marketing ruse to dupe consumers into parting with cash for little benefit.

Ask a service engineer's advice

A local general machine-fixer usually has no vested interests and will chat to you about which machines he is most called out to fix and which machines are hopeless. My local engineer told me that Miele vacuums are, in his opinion, the best and that they also run a cheap collect-and-deliver repair service at a fixed rate which works out cheaper than his own call-out rate.

• Miele, 01235 554455, www.miele.co.uk

In addition, phone the company's repair line before buying to see if it is constantly engaged, and how many other makes it deals with.

Buy American machines with caution

Yes, they are attractive and trendy, but they may have expensive follow-on costs. I had to throw away my American top-loading washing machine after two years because I could not get through to the main switchboard to order a repair and was told by every independent repair firm that they could not get spares. I was actually relieved to see it go, as it did not have a washing powder dispenser – you had to sprinkle powder on top of clothes – and the family clothes were covered in yellow and green 'powder burn' as a result.

DON'T put your freezer in the garage without checking that it is suitable. Often today's freezers just can't stand low temperatures!

Repairs

Ultimate Appliance Cover insures lots of appliances, including digital TVs, DVD players and kitchen equipment, against breakdown from £15 per month. www.norwichuniondirect.com 0800 888 223.

Get an architect's opinion for £20

The architects' association RIBA has a week every June called 'Architecture in the House'. For a £20 donation, which goes to the charity Shelter, they send an architect to give an hour's free opinion on any work you may be contemplating, or simply to suggest improvements. It could be Lord Rogers himself! Register online at www.architectureweek.org.uk 020 7580 5533.

Free advice

– www.homepro.com is a great service providing reliable tradespeople to work in your home (0870 7344 344). They point out that you should not get an estimate, but what is known in the trade as a 'price' or comprehensive written quotation, as this prevents costs spiralling later. They also offer a basic contract form which you can download from the site.

– The Guild of Master Craftsmen recommends members from roofers to mosaic specialists and has an impartial conciliation service if things go wrong, www.guildmc.com 01273 478449.

– Dulux (www.dulux.com) has an advice service, 01753 550555, and decorator service, 0845 769 7668.

– The Interior Designers' Handbook (or IDH), the bible of suppliers. Issued each summer, it costs around £95 plus p&p from RIBA Bookshop, www.ribabookshop.com 020 7496 8300.

– The Building Conservation Directory is packed with good workpeople and helpful articles. £19.95 including p&p, www.buildingconservation.com 01747 871717, or check if they are still selling off last year's book at a reduced price.

– Individual Homebuilding and Renovating can answer queries by fax only, www.homebuilding.co.uk 01527 834497, or or write to 2 Sugarbrook Court, Aston Road, Bromsgrove B60 3EX.

– Focus DIY has a helpline, info@focusdiy.co.uk 0800 436436. For period homes, try SPAB, the Society for Protection of Ancient Buildings, which has various cheap leaflets and runs courses, www.spab.co.uk 020 7377 1644.

Grants for doing up period homes

If subsidies are important to you, check what is available in the area before moving. Some areas are brilliant and some have nothing. There are also various support groups according to when your home was built. The Georgian Group, for instance, are on 020 7529 8920, www.georgiangroup.org.uk

• **The Listed Property Owners Club offers members free advice, legal and other, including free help in reclaiming VAT wrongly paid in the past on improvements. 01795 844939**

General advice from a top designer

National Trust interiors advisor David Mlinaric

sensibly told me that if you get the basics of a house right, especially the kitchen and bathroom, considerations like wall colour are merely the icing on the cake. Before decorating, do your damp course, replaster and get pipes, roof and heating in order. Put up smoke detectors, extinguishers and a fire blanket for chip fires in the kitchen. And finally, go to a large DIY store and read labels carefully: you can save hours with a metal paint that destroys rust as you paint over it, or paint that fills cracks as you go along, or one-coat paint, or fungicidal wood fillers.

• **Dulux Realise flat matt is a new paint that is ten times tougher than ordinary paint and has a wipe-off surface. £15.99 for 2.5 litres, 01753 550555, www.dulux.co.uk**

Cheap tiles

Topps Tiles, which sells floor and wall tiles and wooden and laminated flooring, guarantees the lowest prices or gives you the difference in price plus 5% if you find the same tile, cheaper elsewhere. There is a 30% discount for purchases of over four square metres for plain tiles and a buy-back service if you have bought too many tiles. I have found them excellent, even when my builder vanished halfway through a job and I overstepped the twenty-eight day buy-back limit. They say they can take care of tricky tile cuts for you, hire out professional tile-cutting equipment and do your planning free. 0800 783 6262, www.toppstiles.co.uk.

Cheap furniture

– Buy at auction. Try Lots Road Auction Galleries, 71 Lots Road, London SW10 0RN, www.lotsroad.com 020 7376 6800. To find out more about antiques, buy any *Miller's Guide*.

– Craftsmen can make items to measure and to your design, more cheaply than shop-bought things. Find good ones at farmers' markets, craft fairs, county fairs and colleges of further education.

– Garden furniture is very cheap. I furnished my first dining room with it and it was very successful, with a mural of a garden on the wall behind it.

– Antiques are always worth buying, as you can resell them, perhaps back to the same dealer at a profit. Always check the back of anything before buying.

– Make architectural salvage part of your way of life. Rummage amongst the old junk in these vast yards to find old baths – once re-enamelled by motorbike repair shops, who are cheaper than bath-refinishing services, they are worth thousands – old wood for floors, tiles, lighting … pretty much everything. Add VAT and delivery to prices. The Salvo Pack gives you local information on salvage dealers. £5.75 from Salvo, www.salvoweb.com, 020 8761 2316,

which also runs a free 'materials exchange'
service to put people in touch who have things to
swop.

Cutting the cost of home insurance

Get an independent broker to phone around –
companies offering this include Direct Line (0845
246 8000, www.directline.co.uk), CGU Direct
(0800 121 004); Norwich Union Direct (0870 514
3108, www.norwichuniondirect.com) and
PremiumSearch (0800 109 876, www.hhh.co.uk).

You can get up to 15% off by fitting approved
locks and alarms or by being a member of a local
Neighbourhood Watch scheme, free –
www.neighbourhoodwatch.net or ask your
council for details.

**• Those over 55 can get discounts from Age Concern Insurance
Services, 0845 755 0550**

Check your insurance

If you do DIY, check that your insurance policy
covers 'accidental damage': most don't. A paint-
stained carpet typically costs £1500 to replace; a
punctured pipe, £2000. Churchill (0800 200 311),
More Than (0800 98 98 98, www.morethan.com),
Legal & General (0161 838 3100) and Norwich
Union (0870 514 3108) all have standard policies
that cover damage to glass, TV, computer and

audio equipment. You may have to pay a little more – for instance, More Than charges about £1.40 extra per month to cover accidental damage of your home contents, including mishaps like a dog chewing the sofa, and £2 extra per month for accidental damage to the fabric of your building, which would include pipes. Try to get house insurance which offers 'new for old' replacements and adds free emergency and legal help lines.

Save up to 50% on home and contents insurance

You can save huge sums and get better cover by using an insurance broker to transfer from a high street insurer to a specialist 'high net worth' insurer. High street insurance firms tend to overcharge well-off people, assuming that the more they own, the more risk there is to insure. In fact, people who own more tend to have better security, and burglars tend to steal electrical equipment rather than antiques. By transferring to a high net worth policy, one lady reduced her premium from £1,600 to £816. The same year, she forgot to set her alarm when she left the house and was burgled. A 'normal' insurance company would refuse to pay out, but *her* policy did. High net worth insurers tend to have more savvy loss adjusters who make suggestions like mine, who told me to 'forget about buying a new carpet – here's the money to get the floor sanded instead'. There are other benefits, like a free security appraisal.

• Also check Home and Legacy, 0845 345 1000
www.homeandlegacy.co.uk
www.householdinsurancenow.co.uk

Gardening

Keep weeds down by lining the flowerbeds with a plastic dustbin bag, with holes cut in it for those plants you want to grow. Disguise the plastic with earth or gravel on top.

Free or cheap plants and vegetables

'Harvest' free seeds from existing flowers. Dry the heads in an airing cupboard or anywhere warm, then shake them inside a plastic bag. Joining the Heritage Seed Programme gives access to a free seed library of rare or endangered species. You get six free seed packets a year, free booklets, a free helpline and invitations to visit gardens. £20 (£10 for concessions), Henry Doubleday Research Association, www.hdra.org.uk 024 7630 3517.

Become friendly with your local park keepers or people from horticultural colleges. They often have unwanted bulbs or plants to give away. Similarly, if you see a plant you like, knock at the house's door and ask whether you can have a cutting: gardeners tend to be relaxed, generous people. Pop a cutting in water until you see roots, then plant. If you use growing aids, use a hormone rooting powder containing fungicide, like Murphy's, costing under £2 for a year's supply. Roots can get stuck and break inside gel rooting mediums.

Consider joining a Horticultural Society. Get local details from the Royal Horticultural Society, www.rhs.org.uk 020 7834 4333. You can also make enormous savings on basics like fertilizer by joining an Allotment Society as a 'garden member' for a few pounds. Go to the hut on your nearest allotments, which you will usually find open during weekends between 9.30 and 11.30am. Once a member you can buy things like fish blood and bone at cost price, which is about half the garden centre price. Bags cost around 10p extra.

Eschew garden centres in favour of proper nurseries. One lavender enthusiast told me how she drove away with a carload of unusual plants from a proper lavender nursery, having got infinitely more than at a big DIY shack. The Horticultural Trades Association, 0118 930 3132, can give you details of your nearest nurseries and help and advice.

Susie Thomas introduced me to National Trust Plant Fairs, wonderful places to buy rare plants, 'garden jumble' and to get advice from experts, with children's entertainers on hand too. Admission is often free when visiting a house. 0870 458 4000 www.nationaltrust.org.uk and click on 'Things to do and events'.

A trade secret from golf course managers is that the Recycler Mower mows the lawn then recycles the grass cuttings back below the surface, where they decompose naturally, reducing the need to water and fertilize your lawn, and saving you a trip to the dump. £229 for electric (TORO1) or £299 for petrol (TORO2), www.ecozone.co.uk 020 8662 7200, which also has lots of other natural gardening products.

HOMESPUN ECONOMIES

Petty, penny-saving economies are the spice of life and extremely satisfying.

Lakeland wisdom
The *Lakeland* catalogue (01539 488100, www.lakelandlimited.co.uk), is a goldmine of things you never knew you needed…

– Keep fruit and vegetables fresh for several weeks by storing them in Stayfresh Longer Bags. From £3.25 for twenty of the smallest size plus £2.95 p&p, product 1092, address above.

– Lakeland also sells thermal tea and coffee pots, rechargeable radios, steamers and divided saucepans for all-on-one-hob cooking and even a mini pressure cooker. This cooks three times faster than conventional methods with little fuel, this two-litre version is far superior to the great hulk beloved of our grannies. Product 6208, £46 p&p free, address above.

Make your own
– Save your soap ends inside one of those bags

given away with washing powder sold in tablet form. When you want soapy water, swish the bag through a bowl of hot water.

– Talcum powder makes a good dry shampoo for hair. Brush it out thoroughly though. (Not recommended for very dark hair.)

– Keep a vacuum flask near the kettle. Put leftover just-boiled water in it, then you save electricity next time you want hot water.

– Denture cleaning tablets are brilliant at removing brown deposits like tea stains from cups.

– Bicarbonate of soda makes a good dry shampoo for carpets.

– Always add water to the end of shampoo and conditioner or bath foam bottles in your bathroom. You can get another couple of uses from them.

– A clothes peg is the ideal tool to use in order to get the last drop of toothpaste out of a tube.

– Cut J-cloths in half. You won't notice the difference, and a packet goes twice as far.

– Soak a new duster in equal parts of paraffin and vinegar. Store in a screw-topped jar. This will lift dirt from any surface.

– Salt makes a good abrasive scrub for wooden work surfaces and floors.

– Old toothbrushes come in handy for cleaning in corners.

– Cornflour is a good cheap substitute for starch.

– Homemade distemper or soft paint can be made by adding a teaspoon of water and linseed oil to an egg yolk, then mixing. Add any food colour. When the 'paint' is dry, buff with a soft cloth.

Strange but true

There are certain things classified by marketing people as 'distress purchases' – boring things you don't want to buy but need. Toothpaste, for instance. If you want to save on toothpaste, a natural rubber toothbrush which you can use without toothpaste if you want to, costs £2.25. You need never throw it away, just replace the brushes with a three-head pack in soft, medium or kids' soft at £2.60 plus £3.95 p&p, Natural Collection, www.naturalcollection.com 0870 331 3333. Natural Collection, Eco House, Monmouth Place, Bath BA1 2DQ.

Cheap dry-cleaning

Home dry-cleaning kits, which you use in a tumble dryer, merely 'freshen' clothes, which you can do by hanging them on a line in the open air. You get better value from laundrette dry-cleaning machines, which you can either use yourself or pay the assistant to do for you.

Save pounds off dry-cleaning by using dry-cleaners in a different part of town. Even national chains don't have a set price, but rely on people not realizing that the prices are cheaper in neighbouring, less affluent areas.

If you want to get out of cleaning windows at any price...

If you have a high, inaccessible window, or want to save on the hated chore of cleaning windows, and preserve yourself from being one of the forty people who die from falling off a ladder each year, by installing windows that seldom if ever need cleaning. Pilkington Activ glass has a coating that causes ultra-violet rays to react chemically and loosen dirt and deposits, then the glass also attracts water, which runs down it and washes the dirt off. I am not claiming that this is cheaper than ordinary glass to install, but over a lifetime, it will save gallons of buckets of soapy water and elbow grease.

• 0800 527752, www.activglass.com

FOOD

Supermarket sense

– Never shop when hungry, or you will end up buying more.

– Never visit a supermarket in the morning; after lunch they start reducing perishable things. Arrive just before they close and you will be able to speed down the aisles with all the best bargains.

– Never automatically assume that economy packs are cheaper. I once heard a soap powder executive gloating that it certainly wasn't the case with his soap powder.

– Don't, however, confuse these economy packs with supermarkets' own basic economy brands of, say, bread.

– Never assume that things marked as 'bargain buys' are necessarily bargains. Supermarkets pile up items they want to clear quickly into these so-called 'bargain' sections.

– Prepared chiller cabinet meals are *so* expensive and encourage us in the belief that we can't cook the simplest thing by ourselves – or, as one girl said of her addiction to instant microwave meals, 'I can only cook it if it pings'. Shop with courage and common sense. For example, before choosing the lamb with herb butter, consider whether you can't buy the lamb and add your own butter with a sprinkling of herbs, and wrap in silver foil to save several pounds.

– Don't shop at supermarkets for fruit and vegetables – they tend to charge more for these items because they ask farmers to select those items that look the same size and free of blemishes. Smaller greengrocers and markets get the 'grade two' stuff which tastes just as good though it isn't necessarily scrubbed to visual perfection. If you do have to buy fruit and vegetables in supermarkets, you will save money by putting them into bags rather than buying them pre-packaged.

– Sacks of potatoes are cheap but only worth having if you have large numbers to feed. They tend to contain at least a few ropey potatoes and go mouldy after a while.

– Remember your loyalty card. The average family can save over £26 a year with these cards.

Cheap food stores
Aldi (0870 513 4262, www.aldi.com) and Netto (0845 600 0200, www.netto.co.uk) are 'pile 'em high, sell 'em cheap' stores where you grab a cardboard box, shove your groceries in and pay

cash. I am also a fan of Kwiksave, 0117 935 6669, www.kwiksave.co.uk and Iceland, 01244 842842, www.iceland.co.uk

Lidl sells food plus cheap jeans, garden equipment and electronics. 0870 444 1234, www.lidl.co.uk.

Warehouse shopping clubs

Costco, 01923 830477, www.costco.co.uk is a shop for members only, selling food around 20% cheaper in large catering packs. To join you will need an ID card, for instance, as an NHS employee. Clothes and electrical equipment are also much cheaper – similar to airport duty-free prices.

Buy direct from growers and farmers

– From houses and farms with signs advertising eggs, jams or vegetables for sale.

– From farm shops. The Soil Association's *Organic Directory* lists organic retailers, farm shops and restaurants, www.soilassociation.org 0117 914 2444.

– From farmers' markets, although use your common sense: some of these can be a way of offloading old food the farmer can't sell elsewhere. Once it is relabelled as 'organic', it can be sold for a premium, as I once heard a Portobello Road stallholder boasting. The

National Association of Farmers' Markets, 0122 578 7914, www.farmersmarkets.net gives your nearest.

Grow and pick your own

– Picking your own works out much cheaper and many farmers offer free entertainment, for example tractor rides. Send two first class stamps for details of pick your own farms and farm shops in your area to the National Farmers' Retail & Markets Association, The Greenhouse, PO Box 575, Southampton SO15 7ZB, 0845 45 88 420, www.farmshopping.com will give you local farmers' markets and farm shops.

– Grow your own vegetables. If you don't have access to a garden, rent an allotment from your local council.

– Grow your own mushrooms. Ann Miller won a Gold Medal at the Chelsea Flower Show for her mushrooms. £3.50 buys a kit that goes on producing for three years. She is also developing a strawberry kit, so ask about that. Send a large SAE for her catalogue to Ann Miller's Speciality Mushrooms, Greenbank, Melkie Wartie, Inverurie, Aberdeenshire AB51 5AA, www.annforfungi.co.uk 01467 671315.

Buying from wholesale markets

If you are giving a party or have many people to

feed, get up early and buy fish, fruit and vegetables at your nearest wholesale market. They don't refuse you if you have cash, nor do you have to buy vast quantities. For your nearest market, call 020 7987 1118.

Billingsgate Fish Market, London E14, opens to the public from 5am to 8.30am from Tuesday to Saturday. Also try New Covent Garden for fruit, flowers and vegetables, and sundries like wire, pots and ribbon. Open from 3am to 11am on weekdays and from 9am on Saturdays. Free to pedestrians but there is a small charge for parking.

You can buy cheap meat in bulk at the central meat wholesale markets in Smithfield, off Farringdon Road, London EC1A 9LH (4am till 10am weekdays); Liverpool Stanley Market, Edge Lane, L13 2LT (4am till 11am weekdays) and Duke Street Market, Glasgow (5am to 3pm).

Or you can contact a local meat wholesaler through Yellow Pages and ask for a discount. Alternatively, find a farmer and ask them to sell meat to you direct. I buy a lamb each spring which arrives ready butchered in freezer packs. I save money on delivery by joining together with friends and splitting the meat between us.

• **If you want ready-prepared, beautifully-presented cuts, contact a Catering Butcher who sells to restaurants.**

020 7248 1896, www.nacb.co.uk for your nearest

• Check the special offers from Donald Russell, a Scottish butcher by appointment to the Queen who sells delicious meat and fish by the box. Wait for the special prices and free delivery to save around £9. 01467 629666, www.donaldrusselldirect.com

Getting food delivered

Online ordering services, or even telephone services – supermarkets will take phone orders but tend not to advertise the fact – can work out cheaper because you get more control over what you buy. However, you pay a delivery charge of around £5, except with Iceland, who deliver free for orders over £40. I won't say that Internet shopping is fast, because I have often fallen asleep trying to do it all, but smiling delivery men will carry your food upstairs and take away anything you don't like.

Cheap nibbles

Julian Graves sells food that you don't often find in major supermarkets, yet which is often used by professional chefs such as Delia Smith. You will find nostalgic confectionery, porridge oats, shelled nuts in huge bags and spices at prices more souk than supermarket.

• 01384 282700, www.juliangraves.co.uk. 10% discount on presentation of this book

How to get restaurant-quality food at home

Phone a local restaurant and ask them to cook you a takeaway. Pride in the job often leads them to add in loads of free extras, like dressed salads.

Several companies deliver ingredients or cooked food to give you restaurant-style meals at home without having to leave a tip. Try www.dining-made-easy.co.uk, 0845 226 7885 or www.thehungryfarmer.co.uk, 01334 476377. Also ask your local deli as many now offer home delivery services. If you do venture out to a restaurant, beware the latest scam: adding a service charge to the bill, then leaving the 'totals' column of your credit card slip blank in the hope that you will think they have not added a tip and add a further 10 %.

Money off drinks

Working men's clubs are the cheapest places to buy beer.

Always buy at least six bottles of wine at a time, and ask for a 5% to 10% discount and free bottle carrier. Any supermarket or wine shop will offer this. Oddbins and Majestic will also deliver free.

Duty on wine is over £1 a bottle. Cross the Channel to get the same wine cheaper in Calais. Tesco's champagne, for instance, costs pounds less than identical bottles bought in Britain.

Explore the Internet for traders like
www.bargainbooze.co.uk
www.buywineonline.co.uk www.casevalue.com
or www.comparestoreprices.co.uk
If you have a good bottle of wine in a restaurant,
take down everything on its label and search the
Internet for the same wine. You will be
astonished at how much cheaper it is online.

Make your own drinks

You can make very tolerable soft drinks for
summer days by placing slices of lemon, lime, or
apple, or kiwi, or mint, or what you fancy, in a
jug of water. Leave in the fridge for a time to
infuse. These look lovely and taste much better
than those flavoured supermarket drinks at
nearly £2 for a small bottle. You can always wrap
the fruit slices in foil to re-use them for ages.

**• For all equipment and books on making alcoholic drinks, try
Ritchies, 01283 564161, www.ritchieproducts.co.uk**

Free samples of tea and coffee

H. R. Higgins (Coffee-Man) Ltd gives free 100g
samples with orders over 2.5kg for tea and coffee.
www.hrhiggins.co.uk, 020 7629 3913.

Yorkshire Tea offers complimentary samples of its
famous tea, blended for the incomparable Betty's
Tea Rooms in York, and if you're lucky, you

might get a tea cake thrown in. Write to: Yorkshire Tea, PO Box 137, Harrogate HG2 7UJ, or go to www.yorkshiretea.co.uk and click on 'Sample Request'.

Saving money on flowers

To make flowers last longer, treat them properly. Clean vases with bleach, rinsed out well, or the green slime at the bottom will poison the next bunch. Leave flowers in a cool place to get days more out of them. Change their water daily, adding a few spoons of sugar, lemonade, or other sugary substance. Cut the ends of flowers with a deep groove up the stem and re-cut this after two days.

Supermarket flowers tend to come with flower food and a five-day guarantee. For a superior-looking arrangement at home, buy a supermarket bunch and add in flowers from your garden or from another bunch, to personalize it.

Other things to mind when buying flowers are:

– Carnations and chrysanthemums last longest, up to two weeks.

– Don't buy out of season flowers, which are more expensive, or roses, which wilt within hours or days.

– You can dry your own flowers in the airing cupboard or even on a radiator as long as the air can circulate round them.

– If possible, don't order flowers by phone. Florists tend to nudge up prices, saying, 'You'll need £20 for a worthwhile bunch', whereas, in the shop, £7.50 can buy you a very respectable bunch. If you do need to order by phone, don't use networks like Teleflorist or Interflora. Their members charge extra to phone your order to a member in another part of the country. Save by calling Talking Pages (0800 600 900) or trying www.yell.com for a florist near the recipient of your flowers, then phone your order direct to them, incurring only the local delivery charge.

Eating out

Look out for various 'Lunch for a Fiver' offers in newspapers, available when you collect tokens. This enables you to eat out at top restaurants, though I have had reports of poor service meted out to discount diners, so try not to order tap water when you arrive or you may be unpopular.

The cheapest good meals – I was going to write 'god meals' – are in church restaurants in crypts, especially Southwark Cathedral, Montague Close, London SE1 (020 7367 6700) which has a huge amount of simple style and a pretty location. Thanks to Penny Beaumont for introducing me to this.

Also try the staff canteens at hospitals. Not the smart croissant cafes in the reception areas, but the workers' places, opening late to cater for medical staff. Although you don't get the staff discount, you find meals like old-fashioned steak and chips, as well as good ethnic dishes. While at the hospital, you can also check out things like discounts on travel which are open to anyone who uses the hospital, not only staff and patients.

Other cheap and good places are youth hostels, offering brilliant and quite sophisticated food with wine, very cheaply, to all comers, often in interesting buildings. Try www.yha.org.uk or the information line on 0870 870 8808.

My final choice for casual good food is a college of further education. Here, there is usually a cheap cafe for students, and catering students tend to run drop-in cafes for anyone using the college. Ask any student on the site.

Free teas

If you have a Waitrose or John Lewis account card, you can get free teas, cakes and sandwiches at the Waitrose stand at large county agricultural fairs. You are also likely to get superior service: I was waited on by the charming Area Director at the last one I attended.

• 0845 6049049, www.johnlewis.com

Find out about diners' discounts

Restaurant Services is a free advice and information service covering every restaurant in London. Whatever the occasion, from dinner for two to parties for two hundred, they can suggest a place. They say they always have advance news of special promotions and events like food festivals.

• 020 8888 8080, www.restaurant-services.co.uk

Bottomless tea and coffee
My preference for tea or coffee is to sink into the banquettes at top hotels – never as expensive as they look, and the lavatories are clean. A cafetière of coffee at The Savoy Hotel off the Strand in London WC2 serves three cups, the price of which renders it comparable with a single cup from many coffee shop chains. Also check out Porters, the Earl of Bradford's English restaurant, 17 Henrietta St, London WC1. Little Chef offers free refills of many drinks.

Earlybird deals
Don't forget that chains like Harvester and Beefeater offer deals if you sit down to eat before 6pm, or for OAPs, or sometimes family loyalty cards. Check out your nearest preferred restaurant.

UTILITIES: HEATING, LIGHTING, WATER, POWER AND PHONES

Hot water is an invisible drain on your income. Showers use three-fifths less water than baths, with the exception of power showers. You can save hot water by showering at your local swimming pool or health club, and having a swim too, all for a small entrance fee. These days pools often offer other freebies, for example, the use of hair dryers (thus saving electricity at home) and disposable plastic overshoes, meant to protect your feet at the side of the pool but which are also very useful for protecting your shoes in the garden.

Old-fashioned ways of saving heat are valid today. You lose 9% of your heat through doors and windows, so hang thick curtains that sweep to the floor. I hook in an extra lining during winter. Buy foam draught excluder strips from hardware shops for the bottom of doors or a curtain on a portière rod, which is a rod which opens and closes with the door. Stuff a stocking to make a draught excluder, but be careful not to make a room too airtight. Electric heaters burn money, especially fan-style ones. Consider using a portable Dimplex-style oil radiator instead, which stays warm for longer when turned off.

If you can't afford to heat your bedroom, electric underblankets, which you warm up and then turn off when you get into bed, are cheap. Cheaper still is a hot water bottle or its old-fashioned substitute, a warm stone or brick. Pop this into the oven while you are cooking to get hot, then wrap in a blanket and transfer to your bed.

• **Gas and electricity regulator Ofgem can keep you informed of the latest regulations, help you resolve problems and suggest more money-saving ideas. 0800 88 7777; www.ofgem.gov.uk**

Cutting gas and electricity prices

Gas and electricity companies often put their prices up in spring, a fact that you are unlikely to notice because the weather is warmer and your bills are consequently lower anyway.

If you want to stay with the same energy provider, paying your bill monthly by direct debit or managing your energy bill online usually saves you money. But 150,000 people each week save up to £140 annually on their bill simply by switching energy providers, a task which takes about six weeks from start to finish and doesn't involve re-laying pipes or cables. Before changing, ask new suppliers whether they charge different rates at different times of the day and, if you are offered a fixed contract, say for a year, ask if there are penalties for ending it early.

You might save by using the same supplier for both your gas and electricity, but before doing this, check with Energywatch whether their customer service is good to avoid putting all your eggs in one fragile basket. Those over 50s might check Saga Energy to save around £50 a year typically. www.saga.co.uk 0800 096 0340.

• OFGEM (0800 88 7777) has a full list of energy suppliers

• For help comparing the prices charged by different suppliers, find your last few bills, and consult the following services to calculate your cheapest options: Energywatch, the consumer watchdog, www.energywatch.org.uk 0845 906 0708 for a leaflet; www.uswitch.com www.switch.com www.loot.com www.switchwithwhich.co.uk   Simply Energy, 0800 781 1212. www.cheapest-utility.co.uk compares gas, electricity and water rates and digital TV suppliers, satellite and cable, mobile phones and Internet services. 07092 316745

Save electricity
– By turning your heating down one degree, saving £30 annually. Also save £10 a year by turning down your hot water: 60 degrees centigrade, 140 degrees Fahrenheit is best. Adding an insulating jacket to your hot water cylinder saves up to £15 a year; insulated pipes between your boiler and hot water cylinder save £5 a year.

– By sticking aluminium foil behind radiators, to reflect warmth into the room rather than allowing it to escape through walls.

– With a SavaPlug which, when fitted instead of your ordinary fridge electric plug, typically saves 20% of the running costs by matching the energy supplied to the energy needed.

– By installing a new condenser boiler especially if your boiler is fifteen years old or more. These are more expensive, but save up to 37% off your heating bills or £2,000 over the fifteen-year average lifespan of a boiler, according to Energy Saving Trust figures. If it has good controls, you can save a further 40%. You can also get grants: see below.

– By using energy-saving light bulbs which use a quarter of the electricity of normal bulbs and last twelve times longer. Natural Collection gives individually-tailored recommendations. 01225 442288, www.naturalcollection.com

– By installing secondary glazing, which is cheaper than double glazing but still typically saves 30% a year in heating bills. Double glazing can save up to 20% of heat loss, reduces noise and condensation. See www.saveenergy.co.uk 0845 727 7200 for information.

– By not leaving all the lights in the house ablaze as you sit in one room, by going to bed early or by using candles which you dip in varnish to make them last longer (hold them by the wick and don't varnish the wick).

Free grants
Several government bodies and charitable trusts offer grants for insulation or energy-saving measures. You don't have to be receiving benefits or on a low income.

• **The Energy Efficient Hotline will explain how to get grants towards condensing boilers and loft insulation. You must contact them before beginning the work, though, as they stipulate which suppliers to use. 020 8855 5533, www.est.org.uk**

• **The Eaga Partnership will also help you. You can apply for grants online at www.eaga.co.uk or 0191 247 3800**

• **Check if you are entitled to a Cold Weather Payment at www.dwp.gov.uk**

Cheap central heating
Install new fires and heating systems in the summer, the slow period of the year where companies offer special deals and interest-free credit. Large companies usually subcontract this work to smaller independent plumbers and fitters, however, and it is always worth asking the subcontractors how much they would charge without going through the larger company.

Although you can take out service contracts, which are generally reliable, my independent plumber installed my new boiler and offered me a personal servicing scheme at considerably less cost than British Gas's Three Star. Ensure, however, that the plumber has a stand-in who will be available to help in the event of his absence.

Energy-saving appliances

Look for the rainbow label on home appliances denoting the EU energy-efficiency rating. A is the most efficient; G will cost a lot more to run. Also check water consumption, especially if you have a water meter. A machine using sixty litres to wash clothes will save you 5,800 litres a year in comparison to a machine with a standard, eighty-litre wash. If you can't understand the label, the Energy Efficiency Hotline may help. 020 7222 0101, www.est.org.uk

* Hoover's UltraCare Plus washing machines claim 'A+ energy' ratings, saving 10% more than A rated machines. They claim this can save up to £150 when used seven times a week over a period of nine years. 01685 721222, www.hoover.co.uk

Solar heating

A roof-mounted solar panel, connected to an existing conventional hot water system, can provide up to 90% of a home's hot water in summer. The Department of Trade and Industry is spending £20m to encourage people to put in solar heating, and substantial grants are around for householders, businesses and social housing groups to save 40% to 65% of the installation costs. Apply at www.est.org.uk/solar or call 0800 298 3978.

• **www.sunnythings.com sells smaller products like solar-powered lights, water and radios**

You need a real fire against damp

I once lived in a houseboat so damp that clothes grew mould in the wardrobe, until I bought an old cast-iron coal-burning stove called 'The Celebrated Bogey'. One coal fire kept the place warm all day and I cooked meals in its small oven and boiled the kettle on top.

• **Architectural salvage dealers can provide restored ranges. Try Trade Cookers for renovated ranges, Agas, and even restored kettles and toasters. 01548 830 069. Also try Rod Hughes, 01260 22 7641**

• **The best advice about fires and modern coal-burning stoves I have found comes from Croydon Fireplaces, 2 Campbell Road, Croydon, Surrey, CRO 2SQ. Their service is relaxed, knowledgeable and generous. 020 8684 1495**

To Aga or not?

Agas, Raeburns and similar stoves are cheap to heat large homes, because they provide constant cooking and heat your central heating in one. There are knock-on costs, though. Before buying, check the cost of installation, including the concrete base you may need. Also, you have to keep one radiator working all through the year unless you switch the whole thing off and have a separate ordinary cooker for summer. Some Agas now contain an ordinary cooker within the body of a traditional range. Consult specialists before doing anything and ask about smaller less well-known brands, which may have cost advantages. Also check the costs of heating by gas and oil: you may find oil cheapest.

Save power when cooking

A tiered steamer allows you to cook a complete meal over one hob. To save on shop prices, check camping shops for stacked, tiffin-style pans, which cost very little.

When cooking quick things like eggs, don't use thick-bottomed pans as you waste heat while waiting for the pan to get hot. On the other hand, these pans are ideal if you are cooking a large amount because, once the pan is hot, you can turn off the gas or electricity and 'coast' on stored heat until the food is done.

When using the oven, fill it fully, baking oven chips and fish fingers rather than grilling. Think ahead and cook two days' meals together, or, like our grandmothers, only have hot food on alternate days. Put hot food, tea and coffee into vacuum flasks to have later. Once hot, leave the oven door open to heat the kitchen in cold weather.

Microwaves are magic

A Christmas pudding takes hours to boil on a conventional hob but only two minutes by microwave. You can also heat hot drinks in mugs, but be wary of hot handles. Nor do you need expensive special microwave cookery apparatus, just sturdy plastic containers like margarine tubs, whose lids save the need to waste clingfilm.

A very fast cooker

Sharp's R-90GCK oven cooks up to five times faster than conventional ovens, using something called 'impingement heat transfer' to super-heat the oven and reduce baking time without drying the food. A 2.25kg chicken, for example, takes two hours and twenty minutes in a regular oven but only thirty-six minutes with this oven. The downside is that it costs around £600.

• 0800 138 9908 or www.sharp.co.uk for stockists

Induction cooking

Induction is the most heat-efficient way of cooking because it heats the pan only, not the surrounding hob. Powered by electricity, it is as instantly responsive as gas and about 30% more efficient than radiant hotplates or gas burners. You usually don't need special saucepans. As the technology is so new, induction hobs are costly, but prices will come down in time. Also check that the hobs are easy to control – I have seen some that require you to stab repeatedly at the control panel in order to reach full power, rather than increasing automatically as you press down.

• For more information, try 01692 406850 or www.ripples.co.uk/induct.html

Water

• www.buy.co.uk works out whether you can save pounds by installing a water meter or not

• WaterPower (0845 758 1658) is the regulator for the water companies. www.ofwat.gov.uk contains the latest regulations and news. For instance, some companies slash your bill if you have a water butt collecting rainwater in the garden. Most water suppliers will send you a free 'water hippo' to put in your cistern to save water with each flush. Many water and gas companies (except Mid Kent Water) will repair leaky pipes in your garden, too. Many are reluctant to admit that they offer these services, so you may need to be persistent

• Water charges vary from area to area, like council tax. If desperate, move to a cheaper place

Ingenious water-saving ideas and more

Now that the various water boards are determined to meter as many homes as possible, saving water equals saving cash. Natural Collection is an ecological mail order company with some good water-saving ideas. It sells a 'luxurious water-saving showerhead' for £49 which gives you a powerful flow of oxygenated, reviving water but uses up to 70% less water than conventional showerheads. It fits on any shower or flexible tube.

In the same catalogue there is an 'eco flush' loo handle allowing you to control the amount of water that you use in the loo. From £19.95 in white, also in chrome and gold.

Look out, too, for a bicycle-powered mobile phone charger, solar-powered battery chargers and lights and wind-up radios and torches. Natural Collection, 0870 331 3333, www.naturalcollection.com, Natural Collection, Eco House, Monmouth Place, Bath BA1 2DQ.

Phones

Check your phone bills. I saved over £150 simply by double-checking bills and finding how many times I was double-charged including for mythical 'three-way calls'. If you get an unhelpful response from the first operator you complain to, ask to speak to a supervisor. Threaten to complain to OFTEL, the telephone watchdog (www.oftel.gov.uk 020 7634 8700) if you are still unhappy.

• **To compare the prices of every phone operator, try www.magsys.co.uk/telecom or www.cpi.org.uk which also compares the quality of companies' service, for example, fault-fixing**

Broadband

If you use the phone and the Internet a lot, consider getting broadband. Broadband keeps your phone line permanently connected to the Internet, allowing you access about ten times faster than a standard modem – and you can use the phone line as an ordinary line at the same time, saving money on a second line rental. Shop around for various tariffs and try to find a free connection deal to save around £60.

For very quick services, see www.freedom2surf.net/ads and www.internet-central.net or try www.dslreports.com/tools to optimize your broadband connection.

If you open a PlusNet account, and friends and colleagues sign up to PlusNet on your recommendation, you can earn from 50p to £6 monthly. See the 'my referrals' section at www.plus.net.

Ordinary phone tariffs

For those with two lines, there is a new BT tariff,
Together. Option 1 charges £11.50 per line on
direct debit, then 3p per minute (5p minimum
charge) from 8am to 6pm and 6p per national call
up to an hour from 6pm till 8am, and all
weekend. Option 2 costs £17.50 for the same
daytime rate, and offers free evening and
weekend national calls. Option 3 charges £28.50
per line, but national calls are free at all times.
There are other discounts, like the option to make
5p per minute phone calls to various countries for
£2.50 per month and reduced call charges to
international mobiles. Study them carefully and
good luck.

• 0800 243 123 or www.bt.com/pricing

If you pay your bill by monthly direct debit you
can save £12 a year.

BT's Friends and Family offers discounts to ten
numbers you specify. But have you picked the
most-used numbers, for example, your Internet
provider? Check at www.bt.com.

• Callserve, www.callserve.co.uk (2 Harbour Exchange Square,
London E14 9GE) allows you to make calls to any phone in the
world from your computer. The sound quality is variable but the
prices are reasonable, costing, for example, around 3p per
minute to America. Also try Telediscount,
www.telediscount.co.uk

Free answering service

1571 is the number you dial to listen to messages left for you on your phone. It is free, but if you want to dictate your own greeting, it costs £1 per month. Another £1 is incurred per month by 'message alert' which calls you back when a message was left while you were on the phone. (0800 004 800, www.bt.com/messaging).

Be wary of accepting offers of BT calling features such as 'reminder calls' which cost money. Do you really need these things when an alarm clock might do just as well? Also think long and hard before getting a BT Chargecard, which automatically bills your home telephone bill, no matter where you call from, and which costs a minimum of 20p for calls up to a minute.

• **Carphone Warehouse are offering £500 if they can't prove that you can save money by switching from BT to its talktalk service and keeping your existing number. 0808 100 9250, www.talktalk.co.uk**

Directory enquiries

Most services charge a connection fee *and* another sum per minute of the call. The cheapest services I have found are 11 88 88, charging 20p plus the normal call cost from your service provider; British Gas (11 85 11) and Core Communications (0800 298 6725), both have a 40p flat charge. www.ofcom.org.uk or www.mrthrifty.co.uk

allow you to compare prices of various directory services.

The cheapest way to find a number is to grab the phone book, which is still free, and look things up. If this doesn't come up trumps, up to ten numbers are available, free, each day, at www.bt.com/directory-enquiries/dq_home.jsp If you want 200 free searches a month, you must register on the website. Alternatively, search the Internet for the company's website, which should contain its phone number, or try www.yell.com to find its listing.

It might be worth getting a 'PhoneDisc', a CD-ROM containing all the names and addresses in the system. From £43.63 or with more expensive versions for networks. 0800 833 400. Also look up www.bt.com and search for eDQ.

Mobile phones

• To compare mobile phone providers, look at www.mrthrifty.co.uk

• Depending on your call plan, texting can be cheaper than making voice calls. Sending messages from a computer is cheaper still. www.textmefree.com lists the best free providers

GOOD LOOKS AND HEALTH

There is no magic ingredient

Bath salts soften and scent the water, but the herbs or magic ingredient they contain are in too small amounts to be of any medicinal value. Salt is cheaper and a natural antiseptic. Baby oil, perhaps scented with a few drops of your own perfume, an essential oil from a chemist shop, or even rosewater used for cooking (from supermarkets), is a cheap natural moisturizing bath oil. It does exactly what more expensive oils do: sit on the surface of the water, then cling to your skin when you get out.

Save money on expensive skin creams

Don't assume that expensive skin preparations work better than cheaper ones. The makers simply ask for the price that they think they can get away with. I know this because, in another earlier existence, I wrote skincare advertisements. Makers would set the prices for new potions by asking women how much they were prepared to pay, then doubling it.

You may be better off, boringly, by getting enough sleep, exercise, taking vitamins, eating a balanced diet and – my secret recipe for happiness – avoiding boring and vexatious people and unproductive arguments.

If, however, you insist on skin cream, among the best and cheapest skincare I have found are Boots' own brands and the economy ranges from the Co-op Pharmacy. Never buy your favourite shampoo, conditioner, toothpaste or skin cream at full price as Superdrug or Boots are almost certain to have a 'three for the price of two' offer at any one time. Stockpile these items then.

Money off top toiletries and make-up

Direct Cosmetics sells drastically discounted make-up, skincare, suncare, perfumes, nail varnish, gift sets and brushes by post, offering up to 80% off. Owner Bill Doody, who has been trading for twenty-three years, says his secret is buying in volume and keeping overheads tiny. Postage is £3.95 per order, free for orders over £65. Examples of savings include Elizabeth Arden lipsticks which retail at £13 in the shops but for which Direct Cosmetics charge £2.45. There is also 70% off Max Factor make-up and Balmain fragrances and up to 90% off Gale Hayman. Once registered, you receive a massive postal list of what is available. You can't guarantee to find the thing you want that month, but brands vary widely, from Ralph Lauren to Superdrug. The website contains even more reductions, and you

can always ask if you can't find what you want.
Highly recommended.

• Direct Cosmetics, 0157 275 6805, www.directcosmetics.com
www.directcosmetics.co.uk, www.cosmeticsdirect.com and
www.cosmeticsdirect.co.uk

Top quality cosmetics

Glauca Rossi, the top make-up artist, sells her
private range of 100 cosmetics at knockdown,
mail order prices. These were developed for
professional make-up artists and are not available
in the shops. A lipstick costs £6.25, for instance.
She says all her colours last for a long time.

These cosmetics were developed by Glauca and a
chemical specialist, and made by a top
manufacturer who also produces make-up for
couture names you see on beauty counters. The
technical specifications match many big names,
with non-irritant ingredients, not tested on
animals.

Thrifty readers have raved to me about this
make-up. Glauca's label is so cheap because she
uses tough rather than expensive packaging,
though the palettes are generous enough for
everyday use with mirrors and sponge
applicators.

• The Glauca Rossi School of Make-up, 10 Sutherland Avenue, London W9 2HQ. 020 7289 7485

Free samples and makeovers

Go to any cosmetics counter in a department store during a quiet time of day and say, 'I'm not sure about my skin/foundation/lipstick' (even if a man) and you will be showered with advice, samples and offers of free makeovers or skin sessions. This is particularly true of Lancôme and Estée Lauder.

Paul Herrington, of the Personal Beauty Studio at Dickins & Jones, 224 Regent Street, London W1 (020 7287 4947) specializes in private makeovers. A free bookable consultation includes skincare and make-up with unbiased advice on products. He is also a qualified hairdresser and can advise on a new hairstyle, though the cutting is not included in the service.

Space NK (020 7299 4999, www.spacenk.com for branches) offers free walk-in skin and make-up advice on fashionable looks, or bookable evening workshops, £10.

Cheap perfume

Tesco and Sainsbury's savacentres sell perfume and some beauty accessories at reasonable prices.

The Perfume Shop sells all perfume at a discount,

even the normally impossible-to-track-down Chanel or Estée Lauder. If your favourite fragrance has been discontinued, it will try to find any remaining stocks for you or help you to choose a similar one. 01494 539900 for branches and advice.

www.cheap-perfume.co.uk is a guide to some of the best discounts. Some of the shops listed here sell unused tester bottles of scents by Dior, Chanel, etc. at £1 per bottle.

www.strawberrynet.com and www.fragrancebay.com are also worth a look.

Free samples

Perfume counters of any large and lavish store are always good for a free top-up, if you have been travelling and feel in need of a boost of fragrance before meeting someone. You will also find luxurious lotions and perfumes in the lavatories of smart hotels and department stores like Harvey Nichols. If you ask, Liberty's offers free samples in little bottles, from esoteric perfume-makers. Otherwise they spray sample sniffs on small cards, which you can use to perfume your bag or linen cupboard.

• **Liberty's, 210-220 Regent Street, London W1F 6AH, 020 7734 1234**

Cheap beauty treatments

Women and men of all ages can get every beauty treatment – including the latest and most luxurious – free or very cheaply, by allowing supervised students to practise on them at Colleges of Further Education. The only charge is for materials, though I usually leave a tip. What's available depends on the time of year. September is a quiet time, because the new intake of students are still learning, but by Christmas there are plenty of opportunities to treat yourself to a whole day of beauty therapy and hairdressing. The surroundings are usually clean and attractive, with beds or couches arranged down a long communal room in hospital-ward style rather than individually, as in paid-for salons. You have to book in advance and fit in with their suggested times rather than stipulate your own appointment time.

Contact your nearest College of Technology or Further Education, or your local authority can give you a list of places offering a beauty therapy course locally. For example, the London College of Fashion offers all beauty therapies on most days, and they are even cheaper if a first-year student does them.

• **London College of Fashion, 20 John Princes Street, London W1M 0BJ, 020 7514 7483, www.lcf.linst.ac.uk and click on 'visit us'**

A private college, the Steiner School of Beauty Therapy, offers reasonably priced therapies at certain times on Tuesdays, Wednesdays and Thursdays. For the price list, send an SAE. Example prices are special occasion make-up for parties or weddings costing £9.40, de-incrustation facial with galvanic currents to remove impurities at £11, vibro-massage slimming is £11, a manicure is £6 while a massage, facial, manicure and pedicure costs £32.

• **Steiner School of Beauty Therapy, 193 Wardour Street, London W1F 8ZF, 020 7434 4534**

Cheap therapeutic massage

The London College of Massage offers treatment for aches and pains from senior students at about a third of professional masseuse prices. You may have to go onto the waiting list but it won't be long. You get a half-hour chat about your aches and pains before they decide what kind of massage to give you.

• **London College of Massage, Diorama, 34 Osnaburgh Street, London, NW1 3ND, 020 7813 1980**

Health clubs

Before joining, ask if they are currently operating any special offers; for instance, if a member is introduced, the introducer receives a case of wine. Ask around, find a member to introduce you and split the case of wine. It's good for the heart!

How to get a top hairdo for free

Hairdressers are constantly looking for models, both male and female, to have their hair cut and coloured, free. If there is a particular salon which you are keen to try, which normally charges £100, ring and ask. You needn't be 19 and stick-thin, just not mind having your hair pulled around by trainees. You might get the Artistic Director if you're willing to travel further for competitions, examinations and demonstrations.

Appointments are usually in the evenings and take longer than a regular session, though you can get the most fashionable perms and tints.

• Saks is an national salon group often seeking models of all ages and both sexes. Phone 01325 380333 for your nearest branch

• The Toni & Guy Academy in London offers hairdressing for both sexes at two training schools. 'Classic' is your destination for a trim, bob, accepted cut or one colour or highlights. 'Advanced' is more experimental and avant-garde. There is a flat charge of £5 which is waived if you can present a coupon from Miss London or GAT, given out at most big London stations on Monday mornings. 020 7637 0995, www.toniandguy.co.uk

• Mersey-based hairdressing school Andrew Collinge runs refresher courses for professional hairdressers and needs models for free haircuts (no perms or colouring). Expect to be there from 1.30 till 4.30 in the afternoon. 0151 709 5942. You get a quicker, reduced-price cut from the Training Salon, 0151 709 4848

Alternatives to prescription charges

Before paying the £6.50 prescription charge for your medicine, check that there is not a cheaper version sold over the counter. Medicines which can work our cheaper than their prescribed counterparts include Zovirax, Piriton Syrup, paracetamol tablets, Canesten Cream and E45 bath oil, but check that the quantities are the same as the specified by your prescription.

For a lot of prescriptions, take out a season ticket – a one-off charge of £90.40 for twelve months or £32.40 for four months, covers all medicines, even if they are different each time. You need to buy a 'pre-payment certificate' (ppc) from 0845 850 0030, using a credit card, or by post using the NEW FP95 form from the Post Office, or by downloading a form from www.doh.gov.uk/nhscharges/hc12.htm

All contraception is free if prescribed by your GP or health clinic.

If your GP works from a health centre, you may find that minor operations like the removal of moles can be arranged there free on the NHS rather than paying for them at beauty clinics.

Buying drugs online

www.medicine-chest.co.uk is an online directory of medicines and food supplements available over the counter from chemists. It can help you find the right products and give yourself the right treatment as it is run by the Proprietary Association of Great Britain and linked to the Department of Health.

Don't necessarily take out health insurance

Consider paying a regular sum into a savings account instead of taking out health insurance, so that you can afford one-off charges for private medical care, as and when needed. BUPA and Nuffield Hospitals both offer fixed-price deals for private payers, at a lower cost than they charge insurance companies. BUPA will quote fixed prices, inclusive of any extra days you need in hospital.

Surgicare, a Manchester-based organization with centres in Birmingham and London, offers fixed-price operations for hernias, varicose veins, etc. as well as six-months' interest-free schemes. Ask for more information about other long-term payment schemes.

Nuffield Hospitals also offer interest-free loans for a year, provided that you put down 10% of your treatment cost first.

A taxi driver told me this story. A medical insurance company wrote to his friend, who was insured by them, asking him to pay the bill himself for an operation. They would reimburse him, and split 50/50 the money saved over the price charged to them by the hospital, leaving him in profit. It might be worth suggesting this to your insurers.

• BUPA Hospitals, 0845 600 8822, www.bupa.co.uk
Nuffield, 0800 688 699, www.nuffieldhospitals.org.uk
PPP, 0800 335 555, www.ppphealthcare.co.uk
Surgicare, 01494 511911, www.surgicare.co.uk

Pay for healthcare and make a profit

Private dentists charge up to six times the National Health Service fee, and yet more and more of us have no option but to pay when our dentist goes private and we can't find another NHS dentist. Meanwhile, private medical insurance goes up by around 10% per year.

A cheaper option is a cash plan which refunds much of the cost of dental or optician's charges, plus medical treatment, screening for cancer, diabetes and heart trouble and a little cash if you are admitted to hospital. Most of the companies which offer these are non-profit-making, and don't pay commission, so few financial advisors or insurance brokers will recommend them, but it is a trade secret that you can make a profit if you take out the right plan, as you are entitled to payments for having a child, dental and optical treatment, health

screening and physiotherapy, osteopathy,
chiropractic, acupuncture and homeopathy,
chiropody and allergy testing. You can cut
premiums by around 20% by persuading your
employer or union to offer a plan.

• **Association of Friendly Societies, 020 7216 7436, www.afs.org.uk**
British Health Care Association, 0153 651 9960, www.bhca.org.uk
HSA 0800 072 1000, www.hsa.co.uk
Westfield Health, 0114 250 2000, www.westfieldhealth.com
Health Shield, 01270 588 555, www.healthshield.co.uk
Bupa Cash Plans, 0500 000 125, www.bupa.co.uk/health_cash

Free dental treatment

Gnash your teeth at rising dentists' costs by
getting free treatment, including false teeth, from
dental students at a teaching hospital. You must
de-register at your ordinary dentist and register
in the hospital – you *must* check first that they are
taking new patients. If you're in pain, they will
treat you immediately and give you regular
check-ups. But each stage of the work is checked,
so a five-minute filling can take an hour. For
complicated work, you can wait months to be
treated, but save hundreds.

• **For your nearest dental teaching hospital, phone the British**
Dental Association, 020 7935 0875, www.bda-dentistry.org.uk

Medical insurance which does not become more expensive with age

The non-profit-making Exeter Friendly Society (0139 235 3500, www.exeterfriendly.co.uk) does not weight premiums as you get older.

How to see a specialist and have tests fast

Fast Track insurance secures early outpatient appointments for people without medical insurance or a high-excess insurance policy. It doesn't offer full treatment after your appointment, but it will cover diagnostic testing like X-rays and blood tests. Premiums from £16.15.

- PHC 01923 770 000

How to get cheaper health insurance

HealthNow is low-cost insurance which covers medical diagnosis and treatment only when the NHS makes you wait, including things like heart bypasses, but excluding cancer. See www.doh.gov.uk/waitingtimes for more information about the conditions you would have to wait for.

The premiums start at £9.95 a month and go up to £62.29 for age 84 and over, and they only increase every five years.

- 0800 328 4448 or 0800 028 0050

See a GP at home within an hour

If you are self-employed or caring for children, sick leave can be difficult. You can see a doctor at walk-in clinics in major railway stations, but I tried this and was disappointed when the form filling took longer than the consultation. You may find a fast visiting GP service, for which you pay a fee, by looking in your local Yellow Pages under Doctors, Medical.

DoctorCall is a service which will send a GP to you in the M25 area, www.doctorcall.co.uk 07000 372255.

For general, free advice, you might try NHS Direct, which offers a call back from a qualified nurse or doctor. I cannot really recommend this service, however, as each time I have tried to use it, it has either given the opposite of the right information; or advised me to go to hospital – which I could have done an hour earlier if I had not waited for their return call. www.nhs.uk or www.nhsdirect.nhs.uk 0845 46 47.

For advice on minor ailments including stress and colds, and men's health, see CHIC, www.chic.org.uk (Consumer Healthcare Information Centre).

Free new drugs

If you want help with a specific condition, ask your consultant or GP to find out who are the experts in the field. If necessary, look up the British Medical

Journal in reference libraries or phone their editorial team. Call or write to this expert at their hospital and ask if there are any trials you can take part in. This is the way to get the first use of new drugs. However, you must bear in mind that they may not work, of course, and may have potentially serious side effects.

Any large teaching hospital will want people for drugs and treatment trials, sometimes fit, sometimes not. Call and ask or go into the hospital and read all the notice boards until you find an appeal for people. Usually they pay as well as covering your expenses.

Free contact lenses

Contact Lens Research Consultants tries out new contact lenses for major makers. They are always seeking volunteers to test lenses in clinical studies, at their London headquarters, including people who need bifocals, astigmatism or disposable lenses. All lenses are free, and come with cleaning solutions, and sometimes there is an incentive payment too – perhaps £200 for ten check-up visits. 020 7630 9124.

Free eye examinations

Sometimes you find these thrown in at big glasses chains like Specsavers, 01481 236000, www.specsavers.com and if you are on income support, diabetic, suffer from glaucoma or have a family history of this, are under 16 or over 60, or a student under 19, eye examinations are free.

Free homeopathy and alternative therapies

You can get homeopathic treatment and alternative therapies including osteopathy, free on the National Health Service. Ask your GP to refer you. If they refuse, talk to your local Community Health Council or MP.

The Royal London Homeopathic Hospital has staff qualified in conventional medicine who treat thousands of patients, including hundreds of inpatients, each year, with all mainstream medical techniques and drugs plus complementary therapies like Iscador therapy (mistletoe extract) for cancer sufferers, acupuncture and osteopathy. As with ordinary drugs, the standard NHS prescription charge applies. You don't pay for the homeopathic medicine if you have normal NHS exemptions.

• Greenwells Street, London W1W 5BP, 020 7391 8833,www.rlhh.org.uk

• Also try the Homeopathic Hospital, Tunbridge Wells, Kent TN1 1JU, 01892 632801

• To check if there are any homeopathic hospitals in your area, ask the British Homeopathic Association, 0870 444 3950, www.trusthomeopathy.org

Nursing and care homes

Broadly speaking, people with assets of under £12,000 get full funding for their care. Those with over £19,500, including their home, must fund their own care. However, your home is not counted as an asset if a partner of any age, relative over 60, an incapacitated relative or child under 16 whom you maintain, still lives there.

There are other instances in which the local authority may have to pay for your care, for instance, some provisions of the Mental Health Act. The Nursing Home Fees Agency (NHFA) provides free advice about getting care and paying for it, and will help you understand the rules. 0800 998 833. Also consult the Age Concern information line, 0800 00 99 66 and Help the Aged care fees advice, 0500 76 74 76.

If you do have to sell your home to pay for care, or you have savings, check an 'immediate needs annuity' or 'immediate care plan', giving you regular income for life. This is different from a regular annuity because it is paid direct to the care home and is therefore tax-free. Quotes vary widely so get more than one.

FASHION

Clothes, like people, grow more interesting with age. A neat mend is an honourable thing. To renew worn-out areas, buy iron-on leather patches and replacement pockets from old-fashioned haberdashers.

Before discarding clothes, remove buttons and ribbons, which can be re-used, for example, for gift wrapping. Clothes should be torn up for the ragbag but don't include seams or hard bits like pockets, or you may scratch the furniture when polishing with the rag.

I buy many clothes from charity shops in posh areas and car boot sales. The Duchess of Devonshire confided to me that she buys many clothes from sellers in tents at agricultural shows where you get very good quality items, cheaply. You get the chance to buy the best clothes from charity shops and jumble sales by turning up to help for a few hours, as well as a staff discount.

When buying clothes for men, Scotland is best, where they make things to last.

Fashionable clothes for less

Oxfam Originals is Oxfam's fashionable clothes
chain for men and women. There are four shops in
London and Manchester. Expect to pay £35 for a
sheepskin coat and up to £50 for a leather jacket.
Jeans and couture ball gowns come in cheaper too.
01865 313600 or www.oxfam.org.uk for your
nearest branch.

Bargains at factory doors

Barbara Nadel got this tip from foreign students
whom she lectures to. Every town has its clothes-
making section. Wander round and find the
factories – not the wholesale shops, but the
factories making things. Find the back door, which
is the best place to cadge bargains in any industry,
and ask what they are making. Get chatting and
you may find yourself admitted to the magic circle
of those offered samples of luxury clothes like
coats and baby outfits, at a fraction of shop prices.

Make your own

My grandmother's hand-operated Singer sewing
machine was easy to refurbish, via a sewing shop
(look in Yellow Pages) and I use it to make clothes,
at zero electricity cost. Paper patterns cost a few
pounds and fabric is cheap, especially from
market stalls. There is also the added advantage
that your clothes will have conversational value at
parties.

Lewisham and Deptford Sewing Machines, for example, has sold machines for fifty years. Manager Tony Bulford observes that new sewing machines have dropped in price recently – Brother now makes a good electric model for under £100. The company also sells old Singers, with beautiful inlaid mother-of-pearl decoration, at £20 to £30, while treadle models, worked with your feet, start at £40.

If you want to make curtains and upholstery, take evening classes to help you. An old Singer electric industrial model costs around £100 and some people buy them to re-upholster their cars.

● **For branches, call 020 8692 1077, www.sewingmachinesuk.co.uk**

Dry-cleaners will sew too

You can get a coat re-lined through your local dry cleaner for about £20. They will also add new zips for around £6.50, extending the life of all sorts of good clothes whose trimmings fail them. Dry-cleaners usually know local seamstresses who will make up things from paper patterns, take existing clothes out, up or down, and cut a dress into a skirt for a few pounds – much cheaper than glamorous dressmakers.

If you buy anything expensive at a clothes shop, they will usually alter it to fit free of charge – but only if you ask at the time.

A new lease of life for clothes

Dyeing clothes can restore them, make them fashionable or cover stubborn stains, adding at least two terms' wear to faded school sweatshirts. A packet of Dylon costs around £4.50 from Woolworths.

• Dylon consumer advice line, 020 7663 4296, www.dylon.co.uk

Army surplus and camping shops

These sell the cheapest clothes. I recommend Laurence Corner in London, where I once bought a specimen jar for 50p to use as a vase, identical to those seen later in a Chelsea shop at a pricier price.

• Laurence Corner, 62 Hampstead Road, London NW1 2NU, 020 7813 1010, www.laurencecorner.com

A source of cheap fashionable clothes

The final page of Saturday's *Daily Mail*'s *Weekend* magazine is an invaluable resource when it comes to shopping research. Each week it provides a snapshot of the most fashionable expensive clothes, bags, and sometimes other items, and their more affordable lookalikes.

Never buy anything from a mail-order catalogue when it first comes through the door because if you can wait till a few weeks later, you will get offers of cheaper postage, and huge discounts on the original asking prices.

• **TK Maxx are an astonishingly cheap source of designer-style clothes and gifts, with 60% off jeans and shirts.**
0800 600 900, www.tkmaxx.com

• **Also look at Matalan, 01695 552400, www.matalan.co.uk**

Ex-hire shirts and suits

Hire shops sell off their smart suits and shirts when still presentable. Shepherd & Woodward of Oxford, for instance, charge £1 for a dress shirt in the January sale. Ask at other hire shops.

• **Shepherd & Woodward, 109 High Street, Oxford OX1 4BT,**
01865 249491, www.shepherdandwoodward.co.uk

Cast-off clothes

Rich people sometimes buy several garments in different colours and, after trying them on, discard the ones they don't like, unworn. Sheila Warren-Hill is the doyenne of clothes agents. She sells new and second-hand couture clothes from her Highgate apartment, with names like Gucci, Versace and Chanel at a fraction of the boutique price. She is my favourite kind of trader, operating in a generous and personal way, offering food and a good glass of wine to shoppers.

• Sheila Warren-Hill, 020 8348 8282.
For other clothes agencies, look in Yellow Pages

Over 60% off couture clothes, shoes and fabrics

Designer Warehouse Sales is a London-based company offering discounts on over a hundred designer brands of clothes like Prada and Dolce & Gabbana, at twelve annual sales. These sales are used by designers and lingerie companies to sell off the current season's surplus stocks, cancelled orders and beautiful catwalk samples worn once by the model. Women will find the best bargains if they are size 10-12 and shoe size 7, as this is the standard model size.

• Designer Warehouse Sales, 020 7704 1064, www.dwslondon.co.uk

Bargains during London Fashion Week

The end of London Fashion Week sees a second-to-none beano of amazing bargains in the mysterious tents next to the catwalks. After the catwalk shows have finished you can pay a small entrance fee, and gain access to the end-of-season bargains sold off by the various couture houses and small, interesting wholesalers. The reductions are very substantial, and the excellent quality items including shoes, boots and bags of all kinds and jewellery, and wonderful evening clothes and leather jackets. It is my favourite place to buy clothes.

• **For more information ask the British Fashion Council,**
020 7636 7788, www.londonfashionweek.co.uk

Savile Row suits

James & James, formerly tailors to the Duke of Windsor, make properly tailored suits for men and women at a third of the Savile Row price (from £750) using a computer system into which your measurements are fed. They laser-cut the cloth, saving both expense and time. Your suit is ready within two weeks, with only one fitting necessary, thus saving you even more time.

• **James & James, 38 Savile Row, London W1S 3QE, 0207 734 1748,**
www.jamesjames.co.uk

Top quality clothing at old-fashioned prices

David Saxby sells extraordinary gentlemen's clothes, as well as some ladies' outfits, from his shop in Fulham. Phone for the opening hours, which are as eccentric as the shop. You will find wonderful silk smoking jackets, monogrammed pyjamas, beautifully-tailored waistcoats and suits from the 1920s onwards, real gentlemen's accessories from teepees to top hats, and plenty of extravagant clothes like claret-coloured velvet 1970s suits which he picks up on his travels, from forgotten warehouses. All at good prices and, like Sheila Warren-Hill (see above), he operates on sound principles, offering a warm welcome, as well as tea and biscuits, etc. And, if you find a great-uncle's top hat at the back of the wardrobe, it is worth asking him whether he would make an offer for it.

• **David Saxby, 66 Fulham High Street, London SW6 3LQ, 020 7610 6565, www.davidsaxby.co.uk**

A travelling tailor from Hong Kong

Mr Raja Daswanti of Raja Fashions visits Britain regularly to measure clients for handmade suits, evening clothes, shirts, dresses, leather jackets and bags, made in Hong Kong at a huge reduction on British prices, and sent in three weeks. Existing outfits can be copied or made up in your own fabric. A man's suit costs from £159. You need an appointment and to be on his mailing list. I have to add the caveat that returning clothes to get them fixed was problematic.

• **Raja Fashions, 24C Cameroon Road, Kowloon, Hong Kong, www.raja-fashions.com**

Made-to-measure trousers

Brook Martine, 01384 564096, www.englishtailor.co.uk makes trousers to measure, copies existing trousers and can produce couture copies at a fraction of couture prices, all by post, or in person, at their hospitable headquarters, a delightfully Dickensian place at 15 High Street, Cradley Heath, West Midlands B64 5HG. The summer sale prices are particularly good. If you have a child who is difficult to find school trousers for, they will make ones to measure. Although not as cheap as Peacocks or M&S, you can order extras like reinforced knees, and the trousers will last. Another tip when buying trousers for chubby children is to ask for 'sturdy fit' which any good school shop or old-fashioned outfitters should supply. The waistband has hidden elastic which you can let out.

- **www.figleaves.com sells lingerie online and offers a £10 voucher to new customers**

- **www.kaysnet.com offers 20% off their first purchase of anything**

- **For last season's clothes at reduced prices, try www.haburi.com and www.swerve.co.uk**

Shoes

Personally I wear flip-flops for much of the year. They are inordinately cheap, very comfortable, and save the need to wear and wash socks or invest in bootlaces. I have decorated flip-flops for evening wear, as well as more restrained ones for day wear. When they break, a little duck tape over the soles usually fixes them without recourse to expensive cobblers. Alternatively, save shoe leather and wear and tear on your carpet by changing into slippers or padding about in bare feet whenever possible.

Generally, your shoes will last longer if you wear a pair on alternate days. This allows them time to dry out and recover from stress.

Made-to-measure shoes can last twenty years and are particularly good if you have problem feet. Ask any old-fashioned cobbler, but expect to pay a great deal for the first pair because they will have to make 'lasts' or foot shapes from wood, which serve as an everlasting pattern, and don't be impatient.

• A full list of made-to-measure shoemakers and shoes for special needs can be found in the booklet Footwear for Special Needs, £3 including p&p from the British Footwear Association, 01933 229005, www.britfoot.com

MONEY: LOOK AFTER THE POUNDS AND THE PENNIES WILL LOOK AFTER THEMSELVES

We sometimes scrimp on penny-saving activities, while failing to stand back and look at the big picture. Yet one substantial change could save thousands of pounds.

• **For up-to-date information about the best buys in savings accounts, credit cards and mortgage rates, try www.rate.co.uk**

• **Money Supermarket can compare all the benefits offered by every current account, www.moneysupermarket.com**

Look, no pension
No intelligent person on average or less-than-average earnings should save for retirement, as this disqualifies them from claiming free benefits. You need a personal pension fund of £50,000 simply to provide an income equivalent to the State-funded benefit, Minimum Income Guarantee. Instead, put your savings into things you can enjoy and will appreciate in value, like

antiques, and sell them if you need the money later. You won't have to declare them on your tax form.

Council tax
If you live alone, you should get 25% off your Council Tax, but if other people live with you, you can still claim this discount if they are full-time students, student nurses, apprentices, youth training scheme members, patients in hospital or a residential home, under 19 and others.

If the property is adapted for a disabled person, you pay as if your home is valued at the next band down from its real value. If you own a second home, you get a 50% discount.

Houses being renovated or empty (even if between tenants) and those occupied by students qualify for exemption.

Look up the full rules in a booklet from your local council, and don't fib because they can suddenly send round inspectors.

Reducing National Insurance
The self-employed can form a company and take their salary as dividends without paying National Insurance.

If you employ domestic staff, set up a service

company on their behalf. A nanny taking home £20,000 each year will cost over £10,000 extra in taxes. But if she sets up a service company, she can take £4615 as pay – below the tax threshold – and the money left – £15,385 – is company profit, taxed as corporation tax at £1279. The rest of her earnings come as tax-free dividends.

Switch your mortgage

Ask your mortgage provider to switch you to a mortgage charging interest daily rather than annually. This can save pounds annually, but query it if you are asked to pay a fee for the swop or for the service. Big lenders like the Halifax and Nationwide do it for free. The money sections of all good newspapers contain tables at the back listing the week's best deals.

Play your mortgage provider off against their rivals. When you tell your mortgage provider that you are looking to change (send them paperwork or tell them the rate you are going to change to in order to prove that you are serious) they are likely to offer to match that rate, or even better it. This has happened to me several times.

Don't waste money by repaying throughout the year. If you have a repayment mortgage charging annual interest, rather than daily interest, and you repay more than you owe each month, you are wasting money which you could invest because they will sit on that until the day in the year when the repayment is due. Phone the mortgage company and ask which day of the year they use to repay the annual mortgage, checking when any extra payments need to be received, in order to erode your total debt. See page 126 for more on mortgages charging interest by the day.

Use your tax allowances

Employees with partners who are not working, or higher tax payers with a partner who pays a lower rate of tax, can switch money from savings and investments into the partner's name and use their tax allowance to save up to 66.67% in tax.

• www.paylesstax.co.uk can give you more hints.
So, surprisingly, can www.inlandrevenue.gov.uk

Cheap life insurance

When you get a mortgage, you are obliged to take out life insurance in order to cover the loan in the event of your death. Most people take out life insurance for the full amount when they first get a mortgage, overlooking the fact that this debt will gradually decrease as you pay off the loan. To save on life insurance, buy a policy whose payout decreases over time. Insurance broker LifeSearch claim to 'almost certainly beat' quotes from other companies for the same cover.

0800 316 3166, www.lifesearch.co.uk. Also try
www.cavendishonline.co.uk.

Get an independent financial advisor

In my opinion you are best off paying financial
advisors by the hour. 'Free' advisors are usually
earning commission from the companies they
recommend and may therefore have vested
interests. On the other hand, firms linked in to
networks can use their buying power to get
better deals.

• 0800 085 3250, www.unbiased.co.uk, provides free
information and details of local IFAs

• Members of the Institute of Financial Planning are all
'pay-as-you-go' independent advisors. Ask for the Registry.
0117 945 2470, www.financialplanning.org.uk

• Also try www.ifap.org.uk

• For unbiased, free advice, try www.bbc.co.uk/business/money
or www.moneysavingexpert.com

You do not necessarily save money by cutting
out a financial advisor and going direct to a
savings provider. Companies build in the
advisor's commission and don't reduce their
prices when selling direct, so you are just giving
them more profit and sacrificing the protection
you would get from a middle man if things go

wrong. But other companies offer discounts or may split the commission with you if, say, you change pensions, so that you could end up getting money back on the deal.

Dealing with tax inspectors

If you have trouble paying your tax, call your Inland Revenue office and suggest a definite date by which you will pay. If you have been a reliable payer in the past, they will normally grant you extra time. They will also accept up to three post-dated cheques (which could be for varying sums) for your dues, as long as the first one is instantly cashable.

Not many people know that different tax inspectors will offer different deals. If you don't like what you hear, politely ask for time to consider it then phone in again and ask to talk to someone else or a supervisor.

• TaxAid is a small charity offering free independent advice on tax debt to those who can't afford to pay for it. In one case, a man in hospital was threatened with an £11,000 bill until TaxAid reduced it to £2,000 to be paid by instalments. In comparison, the Citizens

Advice Bureau doesn't have this specialist knowledge and the Inland Revenue is not independent. 020 7803 4959, www.taxaid.org.uk

Avoiding inheritance tax

There is a complex way of avoiding inheritance tax involving changing ownership of a shared home from joint tenancy to tenants in common and setting up a trust. You will need advice from an estate-planning specialist solicitor, accountant or tax expert.

• The Society of Trust and Estate Practitioners has specialist knowledge of inheritance tax. Call 020 7763 7156 for members near you. David Aaron Partnership publishes a guide to trusts. 01525 874081

Saving money on credit cards

If you repay your credit card balance in full each month, consider a credit card that offers cashback in the form of 1% on all you spend. www.moneysupermarket.com gives you the current best deals.

In the interests of avoiding debt, don't allow yourself to be seduced by advertisements for credit cards with low interest rates. If you do decide to apply, however, and are accepted, check that you have actually received the advertised rate. Research from Egg, the online bank, suggests that many of the APRs, the annual percentage rates, quoted by adverts are granted to a fraction of applicants, the ones with the best credit ratings. One in ten researchers was offered the lowest rate – with Capital One the best performer – while just 4% of those applying for a Barclaycard were offered the best deal. Also check whether the cheapest rates only apply to people managing their accounts online.

Before paying bills with a credit card cheque, often advertised as having a lower interest rate than most credit cards charge, ensure that the 'handling charges' are capped. Normally fees are 1.5% to 2%, and are capped at £30, but some have no higher limit, so a £2,000 cheque might therefore cost £40 to write.

Mortgages that charge interest daily not annually

Called offset accounts, these combine a mortgage, savings account, credit card and current account, deducting your debts from your savings or monthly pay and charging you interest only on the balance. However, they typically charge more interest than conventional mortgages, so they are worthwhile only if you have large bonuses coming in.

Shareholders' perks

129 companies nationwide offer these – and to get many perks, you just have to hold one share.

A single share in Eurodisney, Disneyland (28p at the time of writing) will net you up to 50% discount on theme park admission, as well as 10% off hotel rooms. One share in the Hilton Group gives you 15% off most room rates and food and drink. De Vere hotel shareholders receive 35% off top hotels and 20% off the group's Village and Greens Leisure Clubs.

If you travel regularly, it may be worth buying shares in certain travel companies purely for the perks. Buy a thousand Eurotunnel shares and you get 30% off three return journeys a year. The saving can pay for the shares. If you hold 600 P&O 5.5% preference shares (not ordinary ones), you can get up to 50% off the Dover to Calais trip and you also receive an income from the shares.

For more advice on this subject, see the free Barclays Guide – Barclays Stockbrokers are enthusiastic about claiming these perks for you – try 0845 777 7300, or visit the website of www.hargreaveslansdown.co.uk, 0845 345 9880.

Claiming money due to you

Government information sources can be scandalously reluctant to give taxpayers information about allowances and benefits. As a result, £4.5 billion goes unclaimed. Some benefits are not even means-tested, but available to everybody.

Examples include, mothers of pre-school children are usually entitled to a Nursery Education Grant, free payment for up to five nursery sessions weekly (two and a half hours per day) for thirty-three weeks of the year – a benefit claimed on their behalf by nurseries but only at the mother's request. For information try the Maternity Alliance, 020 7490 7638, www.maternityalliance.org.uk or the Children's Information Service, 020 8464 0276. Also, people over 65 who need help with their personal care are entitled to Attendance Allowance, a non-means-tested variable sum depending on the level of need, to pay for carers. The Citizens Advice Bureau will help you fill out the forms to apply for this. Look in the phone book for your local branch or try www.citizensadvice.org.uk.

• **For more information, try 0808 800 6565**
www.taxcredits.inlandrevenue.gov.uk or
www.helptheaged.org.uk/adviceinfo/infopoint

• **Also any asylum seekers' charity such as Asylum Aid,**
020 7377 5123, www.asylumaid.org.uk will know the rules about
benefits which are so hard to get out of official channels. I
suggest calling on the pretence that you are a friend of an asylum
seeker seeking information on the person's behalf about what is
available for them

Are you heir to a long-lost fortune?

You always knew you were really a prince or princess, stolen at birth by gypsies, didn't you? Banks and similar places hold billions of pounds in old, forgotten savings. The Unclaimed Assets Register, www.uar.co.uk can help, 0870 241 1713.

Have you won a prize without knowing?

Not those mail shots which offer you a prize, most not worth the effort of claiming, but perhaps at the National Lottery. Millions of pounds can go unclaimed. Go to www.national-lottery.co.uk. Also try www.nsandi.com for premium bonds.

Enter competitions

Some people manage to make a living from it, and the prizes are tax-free. www.loquax.co.uk lists competitions and has tips on writing slogans and tie-breakers. Free lottery website www.bananalotto.co.uk gives out £300,000 a year in prizes.

Rent your home as a TV or film location

It need not be pretty nor grand and daily fees can be from £400 to £10,000. One entire street in Greenwich makes an income from films which it has used to improve the area with hanging baskets and the addition of a children's playground. It helps to have parking for film equipment lorries, transport links and flats for short-term rent to accommodate actors and staff nearby.

To put your house up as a location, don't pay a 'location finder' firm – some ask for around £200. There are plenty of free agencies, including a 'location officer' in local councils. Try www.locations-uk.com, 020 8393 2423 www.oic.co.uk, 020 7419 1949 www.highexposure.co.uk or FPD Savills estate agents, 0160 322 9234. Also try www.ukfilmcouncil.org.uk, 020 7861 7861 and ask for one its twelve local film location agencies depending where you live. If your property is haunted, www.frightnights.co.uk may pay to hold a party there.

• **Because having a film crew into your home is disruptive, get a contract from a solicitor with experience in this area. For further advice, contact the UK Film Council, 020 7861 7861**

Get a lodger

Under the Rent a Room scheme, if there is a connecting door between your home and a lodger's room, even if permanently locked, you can take up to £4,250 a year in rent without paying tax. Thanks for this information go to Nicola Williams, my accountant at Wilson Wright and Co.

• **See the Inland Revenue's leaflet, IR87, from the Inland Revenue as named in various places above**

Pawn your valuables

We think of pawnbrokers, distinguished by the three golden balls outside their shops, as quaint remnants of a time gone by, but they are useful if you need anything from £5 to £5,000 fast. Their terms can be better than bank loans because there are no long waits for acceptance or early payment penalties. You pay interest each month, which is higher than credit card interest, however, they don't charge interest on the interest, as credit card companies do. Pawnbrokers are regulated by the Consumer Credit Act, so should conduct their business legally.

Pawning a valuable, like a ring, car, TV, painting or computer, involves giving it to the pawnbroker in exchange for cash. You have to repay the cash with interest within six months or the broker keeps the item. Before he/she sells it on, you will receive a warning letter, and he/she must send you the balance of the profit, after deducting your loan and interest.

Know how much you want to borrow. 'Can you lend me £50 (for example) on this?' is the question to ask. The broker will ask for ID like a driving licence, establishes that you are not handing over stolen goods and gives you a contract. Avoid those who charge a 'setting-up fee'.

• **Harvey and Thompson is a reputable national chain, 020 7928 0382. The National Pawnbrokers Association will give you a list of members and sort out grievances. 020 7242 1114, www.thenpa.co.uk**

Be paid for giving your opinion

Contact market research companies to take part in a focus group. You are paid around £25 and a few glasses of wine to give your opinion on a particular topic. Try National Opinion Polls, www.nop.co.uk 020 7890 9000 to register.

E-research and e-polling are increasingly lucrative to take part in. www.gozingsurveys.com pays £25 cash or the equivalent in amazon vouchers but make sure that you click on your country to ensure that you are paid in sterling.

A wonderful and important high-paid job

Government advisory boards have 30,000 part-time paid jobs annually which regularly fall vacant. These include working on boards of trade, hospital boards, obscure and joyous jobs like 'The Government Hospitality Advisory Committee for the Purchase of Wine'. One of the best-paid jobs I saw advertised was one on a committee for the low-paid, sitting several times a month and netting over a hundred pounds per meeting – though you have to read paperwork before and after the meeting.

These jobs tend to go to people in the same obscure political circles, and professional committee-sitters-on, simply because these people *know* about them. There are people called 'portfolio workers' who run from committee to committee, picking up a few hundred pounds here and there, then go on to become professors of business ethics and similar sinecures. But the government is trying to widen its catchment area of applicants, particularly to groups it regards as socially excluded, such as ethnic minorities and women.

The job of sitting on committees is not as exalted as it might at first appear: for example, you might have first-hand knowledge of a trade which can make you the only practical or experienced person on an advisory board. I have met a hospital cleaning lady who ended up heading her health authority. You should also be able to fit these positions around a regular job, as most employers would be delighted to have such an influential and high-flying employee.

You can 'nominate' yourself, which means going onto a general register to show that you are interested; or you can target particular posts. Most of those on the arts or heritage side are not paid, except for expenses, so check whether your post is paid. Don't imagine that applying is easy or that they will receive you with open arms, no matter how well-qualified you are. Be very persistent, from start to finish.

• **Try: The Office for the Commissioner for Public Appointments, 020 7276 2625, www.ocpa.gov.uk**
The Public Appointments Unit, 0845 000 0040, www.quango.gov.uk 020 7276 2489 or 2483, email public.appointments.unit@cabinet-office.gov.uk

the Quango website: www.cabinet-office.gov.uk/quango
NHS Appointments Commission, 0113 254 6452;
The Women and Equality Unit, 020 7273 8880,
www.womenandequalityunit.gov.uk
The Foreign and Commonwealth Office, 020 7008 0804,
www.fco.gov.uk

Mystery shopping

Become an undercover consumer assessing
service standards and checking prices in shops.
Fees depend on the job. Try MacPherson Mystery
Shopping, 01484 643257,
www.macphersonmysteryshopping.co.uk

Modelling

Not the fashion kind, but art colleges pay all sorts
of people a little – perhaps £5 an hour – to pose
for students in two and a half hour sessions.
Contact your local college to sign up.

Sell things

Places which don't charge you to advertise
something for sale include most local free papers,
Loot (0870 043 4343, www.loot.com) and most big
supermarkets.

National second-hand shops

Anything that can be tested, to make sure that it

works, including CDs, will be bought by Cash Converters, a national chain, 020 7381 6046, www.cashconverters.co.uk or Cash Generator, 01204 574444.

Alternative finance

It is an unfortunate reality of financial life that the poorest people are given the highest rates of interest. While the credit providers argue that this is because they are most likely to default, regrettably these high rates make them all the more likely to do so.

Credit unions are non-profit-making co-operatives, which pay interest on members' savings and provide low-cost loans. They are usually run by volunteers and provide financial aid to people who might otherwise be excluded or become victims of loan sharks. They are regulated under the Financial Services Authority so that if anything goes wrong, there is the safety net of the Financial Ombudsman and Financial Services Compensation Scheme.

You can set up a credit union or find one in your area through the Association of British Credit Unions, (0161 832 3694, www.abcul.org).

Proshare investment clubs

These are groups of friends or colleagues who aim

to make money for themselves by playing the stock market. Everyone puts in the same sum each month. There are simple rules and stockbrokers offer cut-price deals. You will need the ProShare manual for £29.50 including p&p (020 7220 1730), which includes a year's free membership – worth £34.50 – of the organization. Some stockbrokers give you the manual free of charge if you sign on with their dealing service.

• Try Barclays Stockbrokers, 0845 777 7300 or Idealing, www.idealing.com which charges a flat rate of £10 per trade and £5 per quarter

Asking is free – charity grants

A friend of mine was left penniless, but educated both her children in top public schools with the aid of obscure charities. She adds that even Eton has subsidized places but that most people don't think of applying. Approach the school of your choice direct, and ask.

If you hit hard times, there are all sorts of funds to help. The *Charities Digest* lists all British charities and what they do. There are funds for the daughters of clergymen in Yorkshire; lots of help for the families of travelling salesmen; and charities like the Theatrical Ladies' Guild helping anyone who has ever worked in the theatre, even if they were merely selling programmes. Look up the *Digest* in a reference library, or buy it for

£24.95 plus £2.50 p&p from 020 7490 0049, www.thanet-press.co.uk. You can find the *Charities Digest* on www.amazon.com (editor Claudia Rios, ISBN 1857830059). As it is a 'hard to find' book, Amazon adds £1.99 to 'handle' it.

Also, ask your union or any other large organization to which you belong, even your employer. There are sometimes charities or bequests lying around to help you, even if you are ill and need to meet emergency bills.

MOTORING AND PARKING

Remember that walking and cycling are your best options, as they are cheap, healthy and ecologically friendly.

Minicabs

Agree the price while booking on the phone. Minicab drivers might otherwise charge the highest rate that they think they can get away with. If you have a regular trip to make, negotiate a fixed price with the office. Also, it is wise to pretend to say goodbye to someone as you get into the cab: I once had a driver who pointed out all the places he had burgled as he drove me around.

Lift sharing

www.liftshare.com (0870 078 0225) has 36,337 members and aims to help everyone to find a driver or passengers to share their travel routes to work, to school or to wherever. The service is free and you sort out costs with the people you share with. Also ask any London borough; try www.northlondontransport.org for example.

Car sharing

The latest idea is to set up co-owned cars between groups of people. Check www.villagecarshare.com or www.studentcarshare.com, 08700 780225, info@liftshare.com to find out more.

Car hire

It may work out cheaper to use public transport or cabs, hiring a car as and when you need one. Easycar, www.easycar.com hires four-seater Mercedes Benz A class cars, by the hour or daily, from £4 plus a £2 transaction fee including fully comprehensive insurance. Book early for discounts.

Don't hire any car without first checking the company's website. At the time of writing, for example, www.europcar.co.uk/specialoffers offered a 10% off voucher.

Au pairs

If you are spending a lot of time on school runs, driving teenagers to social engagements or just want to be able to drink at parties, it might save time and money to employ an au pair for driving. You pay their bed, board and around £50 a week pocket money, saving on taxis and parking. Check your car insurance, however, as some insurers won't consider an au pair part of the family and may charge you extra for a 'professional' driver, as they do for nannies.

You should pay for your au pair to have a refresher driving course over here. A friend, Juliet Moxley, who has employed au pairs for years, offers a significant sum, such as £200, to them at the end of their stay, on condition that they have not had an accident. 'It works, and it's cheaper than losing your no claims bonus,' she explains.

You can extend this principle to other specialist uses of an au pair, for instance, looking after your elderly parent. Having an au pair saves National Insurance and other taxes.

• **The cheapest au pair agency I have found is IAPO, www.au-pair.org a free service which asks for a £20 donation. www.au-pair.org**

• **Others to try include Global Au Pairs, 020 8467 6092, Childcare International Ltd, 020 8906 3116; Au Pair and Student Placement Agency, 01889 505544. Au pair agencies should be members of regulatory bodies**

Forewarned is forearmed

Glass's Guide, from newsagents, will tell you exactly how much any car is worth, new or used, and is the industry standard. Before buying, check how reliable any make or model of used car is, and how much it might cost to put right at www.reliabilityindex.co.uk, 0800 731 7001. Also check The Car of the Year Awards, www.whatcar.com for inspiration.

Don't buy a new car at the quoted price

A dealer's minimum profit is 10%. Expect them to offer a discount, especially as competition is hot. Play dealers off against each other – salesmen enjoy clinching a challenging deal.

Buying cars from abroad

Buying from Europe can save up to £10,000, but the process can take months. Judging from some of my readers' experiences, personally I should be wary of buying a car from an Internet service. None the less, popular sites include www.carbusters.com www.oneswoop.com www.totalise.com and www.virgincars.com should you be interested in this. As the introduction of the Euro and the strong pound changes the situation weekly, for up-to-date advice on buying cars from abroad, refer to www.channel4.com/4car. Look at the 'buyer report'. The EU produces a comparison table of car prices within EU countries. See www.europa.eu.net. If you can get across to France for servicing your car, you can save considerable sums too at authorized dealers.

www.broadspeed.co.uk (01206 263377) is a well-established firm and its website a model of clarity. It can help you to buy a new pre-registered car (three months old) or nearly new car (a year old) from abroad, or a used car from abroad or Britain, or even buy at auction. Fees range from £150 to

£799 depending on how much assistance you require. There are also discount service packages from £99 annually and cheap flexible lease car rental deals for cars to drive for up to two years.

Buying new cars at a discount

Look in car magazines, local newspapers and Yellow Pages for your nearest car supermarket. Also try Trade Sales of Slough, 0870 122 0220, www.trade-sales.co.uk which guarantees to beat the *What Car?* target price on all UK-sourced vehicles. I bought my car there, saving on Internet traders' prices and had it delivered within a week, but did not find it slick or sophisticated as an experience. You cannot test-drive cars and they may not have what you want in terms of colour or specifications, though they do have a huge selection. You inspect the car. You put down a deposit. Once you pay the rest of the money, you can drive the car – for a test if you like, then drive it away. There are overheads to pay, on top of the car's cost, including a £51 'indemnity fee' which no one at TSS could explain, road fund licence, a first registration fee, any other 'on the road' charges and a delivery fee if required.

• Trade Sales, 0870 122 0220, www.trade-sales.co.uk

• Also try www.motorpoint.co.uk, where margins are cut to a minimum and Park Lane (UK), 01420 544300, www.park-lane.co.uk

Other cheap deals on cars

A car broker is like an insurance broker. Normally, they buy company fleets, but they charge nothing to shop around on your behalf. Try Vehicle Sourcing (0186 535 8921).

Brokers advertise in car magazines, so call a few. You are not limited to using those nearby as you won't need to visit them. Ask for a quote on a make, with colour and mileage, or a recommendation within your price range. Test a few similar cars at a showroom. Don't hand over money until you see the car and also check that the broker has legal title to the car. The broker may claim membership of the dealers' organization MAA but you can never be sure. Check that the car is not left-hand drive and that it's driveable immediately without adjustments, such as angling headlamps.

You should be able to collect your new car from a main showroom, just as if you had bought it directly from them, but ensure you have written confirmation of the price first. Also make sure that the dealer has a good business relationship with the showroom and pay the showroom direct. Unscrupulous ones may demand cash at your door, then vanish, leaving you pursued by the showroom who has not been paid.

A company which will buy you a car at auction
Dealers usually mark up second-hand cars at
20%. Julian Trim & Co. are specialists at buying
cars at auction, and take just 6%. You tell them
what you want; they give you a written quote
and order form. You return it with £100 deposit.
They find a car, phone you with a description
on auction day and suggest a likely price and
bidding limit. Contact them on 01747 838888.

Money off motorcycles
For up to a thousand pounds off all makes, try
Granby Motors, 0115 930 1321. If you have
difficulty finding the machine you want, call
wholesaler Jack Glover, 0115 932 6986 for help.

Make money as you drive around
If you don't mind driving around in a car
covered in an advertisement, in the form of a
plastic wrap that you slide over it, you can earn
from £66 to £200 a month. Try www.ad-
wraps.co.uk or www.comm-motion.co.uk
Introduce a friend and earn £25. I suppose you
could always take the wrap off for special
occasions.

Cutting road tax
This is now based on your car's emissions.
Calculate how much your proposed new car
will cost you using www.vcacarfueldata.org.uk

Save money on parking in London

The congestion charge of £8 in central London applies from 7am to 6.30pm, Monday to Friday. You can evade this, however, by parking in Masterpark car parks in Park Lane and Marble Arch and catching their free minibus into Oxford Street from 10am to 6pm, which also runs on Saturdays.

Within the congestion zone, Masterpark's central London car parks offer considerably discounted fees if you visit the theatre, get your car park ticket stamped by the box office and show your ticket stub when paying. You pay £5 for up to five hours and £10 for up to 12 hours. Operated by Masterpark, the scheme is run at car parks at Newport Place, Chinatown; Whitcomb Street, off Leicester Square; Marble Arch; Park Lane; Cumberland Street, Pimlico; Poland Street, Soho; and Spring Gardens, Trafalgar Square.

• Masterpark, 0800 243 348, www.masterpark.org.uk for details

Finding the cheapest fuel

Various tales have reached me of people running their vehicles on cooking oil and the local police pursuing cars, sniffing and arresting them for trying to evade fuel tax. Cooking oils or mixes are not recommended by the Allied Biodiesel Industries, but see www.biodieselfillingstations.co.uk for more information about ecological fuel.

Saving money on petrol, car tax and congestion charges

Convert your car to run on LPG, liquid petroleum gas. At 37p per litre, LPG works out cheaper than petrol as £10's worth gives you over 50% the mileage that petrol does. Also, because LPG is considered a low-level pollutant, vehicles that run on it are exempt from the £5 daily congestion charge. That would therefore save up to £1,250 a year if you drove into London daily.

To convert a car to run on dual fuel, so it switches to petrol if you can't find an LPG pump, can cost around £2,000, but under the TransportEnergy PowerShift programme, you can claim a 60% refund. Look at www.transportenergy.org.uk and www.lpga.co.uk for details.

If you drive a company car, however, your car is perversely still classed as a petrol-guzzler. Check the tax rate you will pay at www.rate.co.uk. You can lessen your tax bill by buying a dual-fuel car straight from the factory. Buying, for example, a Vauxhall Astra gives you the 60% conversion grant on the £1,950 conversion charge, but also lower taxation based on less pollutant emissions. Road tax is also reduced from £155 to £110 a year. As your petrol tank is still in place, your

travelling range is greater than a petrol-only
vehicle.

Avoiding the London congestion charge

www.viamichelin.co.uk gives you routes across
London which bypass the congestion zones and
tells you how much longer it takes.

Electric bicycles cost from £500, evade the
congestion charge, are very cheap to run and
don't need a helmet, licence or petrol. You charge
them from an ordinary socket. Just pedal
normally and it feels as if an invisible hand is
giving you a push. Also investigate the Velo
Solex, a petrol-powered bike based on a 1940s
French model, for which you need a helmet and
licence.

• Solex Centre, 408 Kings Road, London SW10, 020 7795 0175

Check your car's history before you buy

Having a second-hand car's registration
document does not mean that the seller is the
legal owner. If the car was leased, the leasing
company will trace you and you will have to
make up the payments or lose it.

When buying, make a basic check on the car's
chassis number – one imprint of which is found
under the driver's side wing bonnet and the other

at the feet of the driver where the carpet begins.
Make sure both numbers are the same, or the car
has been welded together from two stolen or
written-off vehicles.

HPI Ltd holds a register of all cars, and can detect
those which have undesirable histories, such as
being involved in big crashes, stolen or with
outstanding finance agreements. Tell them the
car's registration number and chassis number
and they will check it in minutes. About a third
of cars they are asked about have problems.
£37.95 online, www.hpicheck.com
£39.95 by phone 01722 422422.

Get your car inspected before buying

The AA, 0800 783 4610, www.theaa.co.uk
charges £36.99 for a car history, £260 for a
superior check, including a three-month
warranty; £199 for an 'advanced inspection'.
I have to say that there are caveats on this
inspection, a bit like a house surveyor who
excludes himself from responsibility for certain
things you would rather like to know about.

The RAC, 0870 533 3660, www.rac.co.uk charges
£189.95 for a road test, history and full report,
with no time limit – they say that if any major
fault is found afterwards, you can go back to
them at any point, although this seems rather
open-ended to me. £139.95 buys a more basic

test and £39.95 a history only.

Rescue services

For the cheapest quotes, see
www.moneysupermarket.com/roadsiderescue and
check the smaller rescue services such as Britannia
Rescue; Europ Assistance's UK Driver Assist (01444
442211); Green Flag (0800 3288 772) and the
Environmental Transport Association (01932
828882). Gem Recovery was recently recommended
by The Sun newspaper as the cheapest. Gem (the
Guild of Experienced Motorists), (01342 825676,
www.roadsafety.org.uk).

You can cut costs by paying through direct debit,
racking up a no claims bonus (with the RAC for
example) or negotiating cheaper cover for a second
car. Over 50s should check Saga (0800 096 4080,
www.saga.co.uk) for discounts; car club members,
the RAC.

Never let the police tow your car off the motorway.
The minimum charge is over £100 plus mileage. If
you break down on the motorway, use the emergency
phones rather than your mobile and the police can
locate you and send a patrol car to guard you.

Money off car insurance

Insurance brokers (try Autodirect, 0800 731 0805,
www.autodirect.co.uk and Hill House Hammond,

0800 056 6666, www.hhh.co.uk/yp) cost no more
than going to an insurer direct, and may know
insurance companies you don't. They can save
you the tedium of shopping around and help you
in a dispute with your insurers because they have
more muscle.

Other ways of saving money on your car
insurance include:

– Keep the car in a garage. That can save you 10%
off your premium.

– Don't use it to drive to work each day.

– Don't drive flashy cars. The insurance is
massive, it is likely to be stolen or clamped, and
no other driver will let you into a queue.

– Get an immobilizer, tracking device, alarm or
deadlock. Check first with your insurer which
anti-theft device will gain you most money off.

– Insure in the woman's name if you are a couple
and add the man as a second driver. Quotes can
be up to 20% lower for women. Try Diamond
(0800 362 436) or Norwich Union's Lady
Motoring (via Hill House Hammond, 0800 056
6666, www.hhh.co.uk).

– If you have two cars, don't lump them into one
policy. If one car is used for commuting, tell the
insurer that the other one is used for social,

domestic or pleasure use, qualifying for a 5% to 10% discount. If your second car is a sporty or classic car, an owners' club may be cheaper, especially if you agree to limited mileage and don't add a teenager to the policy.

– If you have a third car, insurers will assume it is for a young person and weight the premium accordingly unless you tell them otherwise.

– If you have a family car, insure in the oldest person's name.

– If you are young and are changing addresses a lot, insure from your family home. But you must be honest about this otherwise your policy won't pay out.

– Don't use 'any driver' policies. If possible, limiting the number of drivers generally proves cheaper.

– Ask Norwich Union, 0800 092 9565, www.nudquote.com about its new 'pay as you drive' cover, which calculates individual premiums according to when and where you drive.

Take extra tests

Pass Plus is a government-backed driving scheme demanding six hours of observed driving in harsh conditions like rain and darkness. Any established driving school can offer tuition and tell you how to book the test. With Pass Plus, new drivers can secure up to 40% off their insurance premium.

Experienced drivers can take the Institute of Advanced Motorists' Advanced Driving test which, if you pass, means you are regarded as being 50% to 70% less likely to be involved in an accident; that your understanding of fuel consumption will enable you to save you 5% on petrol costs; that you understand how to minimize tyre wear and tear, clutch lifespan and avoid minor dents and corrosion that contribute to the depreciation of your car's value. £85.

Joining the IAM, 020 8996 9600, www.iam.org.uk (£14.50 membership a year) once you have passed the test, gives you discounts on insurance – particularly useful for young drivers aged from 17 to 26 who have not yet built up no-claims bonuses – airport parking, AA and RAC membership as well as free tyres.

Saving money on speeding fines

Check where speed cameras are by visiting www.speedtrap.com. Muddy number plates are common. You can buy the 'flashiest' reflective numberplates called Digitech from www.argtec.com at $59.99 plus shipping. These don't photograph well, however.

Saving money on parking tickets

A little-known fact is that a ticket is not issued until it is placed on your windscreen. If you see a traffic warden next to your car, don't bandy words: get in and drive away fast. If the issuing warden was not wearing a hat, and a hat is part of the uniform in that borough, they are 'incorrectly dressed' and you should be able to appeal against the ticket successfully.

A helpful map service

www.mapminder.co.uk gives up-to-date information on entertainment in a given area, like cinema listings and performance times; and tells you exactly how to reach the place by car or on foot. A subscription to the site costs from £2.95 per month, with a free thirty-day trial. www.multimap.co.uk is also useful.

Servicing

Be clear when briefing mechanics. Don't, as I once did, just say 'Do everything' and find yourself paying to correct a rattle in the glovebox. If you are a woman, it might pay to get a man, even if he knows nothing about cars, to talk to the mechanic. A recent survey showed that men tend to charge other men lower prices.

Get a pre-MOT service

MOTs provide profits for unscrupulous garages
who fail your car for some minor point like a
cracked headlight so that you have to pay them
for a second test plus the cost of the work. It is
cheaper to get a pre-MOT service done at the
garage testing your car. You avoid their charges
for driving your car to a test centre elsewhere
first, and, of course, they will do up the car to
pass first time. Look in Yellow Pages for garages
who advertise a fixed fee, or do not charge a fee
for a second test.

If are unsure about why you failed, check the
rules with the help of your local Vehicle Testing
Enforcement Centre (look it up in the phone
book or ask your council).

TRAVEL AND HOLIDAYS

Do not go away on holiday out of habit

There is a lot to be said for staying at home. It's cheaper, your bed is comfortable, the food will not upset your stomach and you do not have to get up for breakfast or leave tips for maids. Instead, adopt the old working-class habit of Going Out for Days. Short breaks of a few days have the advantage of not leaving you trying to concertina your normal week's work into the time before and after the holiday.

Consider the hidden costs of any holiday

Before fixing on a destination, or type of holiday, consider:

– Does it need extra equipment that will cost expensive airfreight fees, and need to be updated next year? Or can you find a hotel that will loan you diving or skiing equipment and save money?

– Are you going to a malaria area, needing vaccinations? You can get most injections free from your GP: check, before going to expensive vaccination centres.

– Is the exchange rate in your favour? In any case, take a cash sum in dollars with you. They always help to smooth over problems remarkably quickly.

Shop around

We expect a package holiday to include everything, but a recent survey found that the same holiday can vary in price by up to 35%, through different travel agents, whose discounts are bumped up by extras. These can include 'booking fees', which are baffling: holiday companies exist to take bookings, and charging a fee for this service seems absurd.

• Look at www.expedia.co.uk; www.ebookers.com and www.deckchair.com

Check these websites before booking

www.voucherfreebies.co.uk/holidays contains vouchers to download which give you instant money off car hire, flights or rooms in hotel chains.

Join the Rough Guide Travel Club (www.travel.roughguides.com/travelclub) for all sorts of discounts.

Earn money off flights or holidays by visiting www.greasypalm.co.uk. Look under 'fast cash' where Holiday Watchdog offers cashback rewards for genuine travel reviews.

www.rac.co.uk has travel-related offers, even
for non-members.

An Internet hotel booking service to save pounds

Smooth Hound Systems, 01242 529509,
www.s-h-systems.co.uk has over 100,000 hotels
and guesthouses on its books and can find you
a central London hotel room for £59 with
breakfast for two.

Basic value hotel rooms

Never accept a hotel's first quoted room rate.
Ask this ungrammatical question, which
establishes you as an insider: 'Is that the best
price you can do?' They will normally take the
hint and come up with a special offer.

As long as you can do without posh décor,
Travelodge and similar hotels near motorway
service areas furnish basic good value for a
weekend break, sleeping two adults and two
children under 16 for between £25 and £35. One
thing to note is not to buy the food they sell in
reception, as the same meals and snacks are
cheaper in the motorway service area restaurant
next door. (0870 900 1995,
www.travelodge.co.uk).
Also try Travel Inn, 01582 499285,

www.travelinn.co.uk or
Days Inn, 0800 544 8313, www.daysinn.co.uk
HolidayInn hotels, 0870 405060,
www.holiday-inn.co.uk are a few pounds dearer,
but may have a pool and lots of deals offering
free children's meals and stays.

Reduced rates in new hotels
New hotels, and old hotels which have just been
renovated, offer a discounted 'soft opening' rate
for up to three months, to encourage you to
ignore glitches such as the sharp nail sticking
out of the carpet which I encountered in one
such place.

• **Check with the chain of your choice. For instance, Le
Meridien, 020 7025 7039, www.lemeridien.com
Four Seasons, 0800 526 648, www.fourseasons.com
Sofitel, 020 8283 4570, www.sofitel.com
www.ramadajarvis.co.uk**

A free holiday
A cheery phone call from a stranger announced
that I had won a prize – seven nights for four in
the Mediterranean country of my choice, with
flights included. This was Club La Costa, 01702
468782. These, and similar companies, are
usually selling time-share holidays. They are not
simply wanting to give you a good time in
return for your recommendation to a few

friends, as they may claim. The real deal is: you get the holiday, usually in a new, lovely resort. Before taking up your holiday you will first have to attend an 'exhibition' purportedly to collect your prize and discuss the resorts. In reality this is a sales presentation, around two hours long and you must go with your partner. You may want the time-share but if you don't, grit your teeth and grab as many free biscuits as they provide. You can still take the holiday, but normally when you get there, you have to spend more time at a sales presentation. If you can't stop yourself signing up, there is a cooling-off period afterwards which enables you to get out of the agreement if you change your mind.

How to stay in a dream house

HomeLink International, 01344 842642, www.homelink.org.uk has 12,500 members in fifty countries all over the world, who offer their homes in exchange for yours for a holiday. The £95 joining fee gives you an 800-page directory three times a year. The company says it rarely has security problems, but you should check with your home insurer before exchanging homes – visitors are usually covered as 'non-paying guests'.

• **Also try: Intervac International Home Exchange, 0122 589 2011; Home Base Holidays, 0208 886 8752;**

www.HomeExchange.com
www.holi-swaps.com
www.seniorshomeexchange.com

Get paid for going on holiday

Friends of mine, Wendy and Ross Tanton, with two boys of school age, enjoy family holidays in a luxury home in Cornwall – with a well-stocked fridge and swimming pool – and get paid for it. Wendy bumped into the homeowner one day, who bemoaned the fact that regular house-sitters apparently don't like to walk dogs. Wendy said she would treat the dogs royally, and they have been holidaying in princely splendour there since.

You can become a professional house-sitter, travel to exotic locations and, at the same time, save money on running your home. This is especially attractive to single and retired people, but of course at least one person is expected to stay in, virtually all the time. Try www.housesitters.co.uk, 0845 130 3100, for information. www.caretaker.org lists private islands and mansions overseas which require sitters. For house-sitting anywhere else in the world, try www.askjeeves.com and type in 'How do I become a professional housesitter?'

An exciting family holiday

Staying in British hotels can be as expensive as holidays abroad, but there is an unusual campsite in North Cornwall which offers a family holiday in tipis, similar to Red Indian tents. They are ready erected, with cooker and coolbox included and a firepit for outdoors. There are two rowing boats, and you can catch dinner in the trout lake. 01208 880 781, www.cornish-tipi-holidays.co.uk and prices start from £295 per week.

Luxury hotel breaks

The Travel Offers Directory, 0870 077 2440, www.travel-offers.co.uk and The Privilege Pass cost £29.50 plus £3.50 p&p and list over 420 hotels in Britain, the Channel Islands, Northern Ireland and Eire with star ratings, including some stunning ones, at which you and a partner can stay free for anything from a night to a week, enjoying free sports facilities too. You have to pay for breakfast and dinner, but the book tells you the likely cost – from £19.50 daily.

Farm holidays

Farms are unrivalled for hospitality, especially for families, and the entertainment is free and all around you, in the form of animals and chat with the farmer. I have spent memorable afternoons being shown someone's prize pigs or feeding hens and discussing farming. Farm Stay UK has 1,100 working farms to stay on. 01271 336141, www.farmstoyou.co.uk for a free guide.

Romantic holiday homes

The Landmark Trust, 01628 825925,
www.landmarktrust.co.uk gives everyone a
chance to stay in a gigantic folly built like a
pineapple, or a windswept castle oozing history.
This charity restores our architectural gems and
furnishes them plainly but beautifully, offering
them to self-caterers at modest rents compared to
commercial rents for such grand holiday homes.
There are some foreign lets too, mainly in Italy.

Grand country houses

At £15.50 to join, or £22 for family membership (up
to five children), and £10 to £12 per night in a
hostel, or £14 to £15 in London, with reductions for
children and free for those under 5, it's a wonder
that we all don't go and live in considerable
splendour in a Youth Hostel Association mansion
like King John's former castle, St Briavels in the
Forest of Dean. You no longer have to clean the
kitchen as part of your payment. Furthermore,
there is no age limit, there is a friendly atmosphere,
cars are accepted and rooms are clean and
comfortable. You can book private rooms, some
with ensuite shower, and family rooms. You are
given linen when you check in.

Book ahead for the best places, especially seaside
hostels. You can self-cater or larger hostels serve
fantastic three-course meals for a few pounds with
wine and beer. For even cheaper accommodation,

try a Camping Barn, providing basic shelter for a group or singles.

• **YHA membership, 0870 870 8808, www.yha.org.uk**
brings further discounts for shops and travel, including 25% off
membership of the Ramblers Association.

• **Outdoor types should also try Little Beach Hotel, Woolacombe,**
North Devon, 01271 870398, www.surfedout.com, a B&B for
surfers from £30 per night.

Basic rooms for rent
Universities rent rooms to holidaymakers during the summer. Central London charges are under £30 a night. www.housing.lon.ac.uk or check the university offices at the city of your choice.

Working holidays
There are two types of these: holidays where you pay a fair sum plus your travel costs for the privilege of helping a project; and really low-cost holidays where you work in small groups for the fun and friendship of it. For the latter, try:

– The National Trust, 0870 429 2429,
www.nationaltrust.org.uk/volunteering
which organizes around five hundred holidays a year, each with twelve volunteer spaces for those aged between 17 and 60, costing around £55 a week. Projects can include clearing weeds from a

river, goatherding and setting up a sculpture trail, with a picnic lunch and scout camp accommodation.

– BTCV, 014918 21600, www.btcv.org a conservation charity organizing national and international projects. For instance, building walls on Arran costs £85 for ten days. You make your own way to a meeting point and from then, travel, accommodation and food are included.

– Thistle Camps, 0131 243 9470, www.thistlecamps.org.uk organized by the National Trust for Scotland, offers work like barn-building with crofters on remote islands, £150 for a week plus transport to Edinburgh. Trailblazers are another kind of 'helpful holiday' for 16 and 17 year olds.

– Worldwide Volunteering 01935 825588, www.wwv.org.uk has 250,000 placements for volunteers.

– Vacation Work 01865 241978, www.vacationwork.co.uk publishes around forty handbooks, such as Summer Jobs Abroad.

– International Voluntary Service 01206 298215, www.ivs-gb.org.uk sends volunteers to work all over the world from £95.

– Many small charities need volunteers to staff
orphanages or build schoolrooms. A good
starting point is Voluntary Service Overseas
www.vso.org.uk for people aged 17 to 70.
Regional offices are found in the
South East, 020 8780 7200;
Midlands and Anglia, 01214 281614;
the North, 01274 740458;
Scotland, 0131 667 3073;
Ireland, 028 9032 8872;
Wales and the South West, 029 2041 5047.
Also try World Service Enquiry, a charity.
0870 770 3274, www.wse.org.uk or
Jobs in Charities, 0870 141 7029.

Mind how you go when buying travel insurance

The form E111, free from the Post Office, is cited
as the way to insure yourself cheaply if going
abroad with partner and children under 19 in
full-time education. The myth is that it allows
you free medical care in any EC country.
However, it is not recognized in many places
such as Turkey and Switzerland, and using it can
be problematical on Spanish islands and in
Greece. You pay treatment costs there and then
and can wait months for a refund; you don't
usually get all your medical costs refunded; it
does not cover ambulance transfers or air-sea
rescues or bringing a body home; and you need
to start your claim at the time you are abroad,
which can be difficult if you are severely ill.

If you go away with an existing medical problem which might flare up, you need a different form again, so check at the Post Office. You also need to get your forms stamped before going away. You must tell your travel insurers about any existing health problems before travelling or you may not be covered.

Many credit cards offer basic travel insurance when you pay for tickets or your holiday on the card, but this is riddled with exclusions. Take the policy away with you, copied several times and kept in various bags. Some cards, like American Express, have a problem-solving service to help if, say, you lose your money while abroad.

If you want watertight cover, phone around or ask an insurance broker to compare premiums. You can pare down a quote by specifying travel only in Europe, or holidays excluding winter sports, or if you are a single parent.

• **www.moneysupermarket.com searches 1,200 policies to find the right one for you. Remember, cheaper policies often offer less cover**

Skiers
Excluding snowboarding and similar high-risk fun saves 25% off the price of a policy. Check that the insurance covers 'off-piste' or you may waste your money: seven out of ten insurers

don't insure you away from regular ski-runs and at a resort, these are not always signposted, making it easy for insurers to get out of paying for accidents. Supplement your cover by buying a 'carte neige' with your ski pass at the resort, which covers mountain rescue.

Buy travel insurance online

An annual policy, covering all your travel and for all the family, is better value than a one-off journey policy; again you can save by specifying Europe only and excluding winter sports. Phoning each number takes three minutes or so: they are legally obliged to ask you the same questions, so comparing costs is faster on the Internet. For more hints and tips, read www.travellersweb.co.uk, 0800 028 2396.

• **Direct Travel, 01903 812345, www.direct-travel.co.uk**
Churchill, 0800 026 4050, www.churchill.com
Primary Direct, 0870 444 3434, www.primarydirect.co.uk
Thomas Cook, 0870 758 0205, www.thomascook.com
Direct Line, 0845 246 8704, www.directline.com
Tesco, 0845 300 8800, www.tesco.co.uk
NatWest, 0800 331 133, www.natwest.com
American Express, 0800 700 737, www.americanexpress.co.uk
Journey Wise, 0870 845 5555, www.journeywise.co.uk
Options, 0870 848 0870, www.optionsinsurance.co.uk
MRL, 0870 876 7677, www.mrlinsurance.co.uk
NU Direct, 0800 121 007, www.nud.com
Preferential, 01702 423393, www.preferential.co.uk

Post Office, 0800 387 858, www.postoffice.co.uk
Boots, 0845 840 2020, www.bootsinsurance.com

Getting a free flight upgrade

Ask when you confirm your flight and check in.
The two golden rules seem to be to look very smart
and do not have children with you. I was once the
only person in a group not to receive an upgrade,
because the staff saw me saying goodbye to
children at the airport and assumed they were
flying with me.

Guaranteed low prices for flights

RBS Advanta Travel Service say: 'We guarantee
that if you can show, within twenty-four hours of
booking, that the identical flight was available for
less (after deducting any discount), we will refund
the difference.' 0870 904 6060.

Budget airlines

Air Europa, 0870 240 1501, www.aireuropa.co.uk
Air Scotland, 0141 222 2363, www.air-scotland.co.uk
Air Wales, 0870 777 3131, www.airwales.co.uk
BMI Baby, 0870 264 2229, www.bmibaby.com
EasyJet, 0870 600 0000, www.easyjet.com
Flybe, 0870 567 6676, www.flybe.com
FlyGlobespan.com, 0870 556 1522,
www.flyglobespan.com
Germanwings, 020 8321 7255,

www.germanwings.com
Hapag-Lloyd Express, 0870 606 0519,
www.hlx.com
Jet2 airways, 0870 737 8282, www.jet2.com
Meridiana, 020 7839 2222, www.meridiana.it
MyTravelLite, 0870 156 4564,
www.mytravellite.com
Planet Air, 0845 060 6666, www.planetair.co.uk
Ryanair, 0871 246 0000, www.ryanair.com
Scot Airways, 0870 606 0707,
www.scotairways.co.uk
SN Brussels airlines, 0870 735 2345,
www.brusselsairlines.com
Volare, 01293 562266, www.volare-airlines.com

It may be worth asking a friend in the country
you are flying to, to find out the price if they buy
the ticket at their end and send it to you. Or just
call the airline office in a European country and
buy the tickets from them, asking them to send
them to you. Also remember to check flight prices
with traditional airlines too. Keen to keep
customers on their traditional routes, they
undercut budget operators. For instance, Flybe
charges £98 from Birmingham to Toulouse, but
BA charges £89.

Save money by flying as a courier
A one-off job. Couriers used to travel free, but
charges were introduced to stop people not
turning up. You don't get paid, but you get
bargain air-fares, perhaps half price, and a

guaranteed seat on a scheduled service. In return, you collect an envelope of documents before flying and carry it as hand luggage, giving it in to the airline desk on arrival. English-speaking staff nanny you through customs. I know someone who got her air courier cheap fare and had nothing to carry on the day. Couriers are not responsible for the package contents and can't be arrested if someone smuggles something inside.

• **Try Jupiter Service for Australia, 01753 443747.**
Other services are advertised in free magazines intended for Australians, New Zealanders and South Africans like TNT, 020 7373 3377, or look in Yellow Pages.

• **Also try www.aircourier.co.uk, www.websciences.org/dvhpub/bumped.htm**

Save thousands by buying your ticket abroad

If you want to fly to New York by BA First Class or Club Class, for example, begin your journey a few weeks earlier by buying a single, cheap ticket to Paris or Geneva. On your arrival, buy an open return ticket from Paris or Geneva to New York which flies via Heathrow. An open return means you don't have to fly on to New York immediately but instead of paying £6,577 or £3,630 for First or Club Class respectively, as you would if you stayed in Britain and bought a return from Heathrow to New York, you pay £4,086 or £1,291 from Geneva or £3,290 or £1,556 from Paris. You return to Heathrow on the short flight home, using the ticket you have just bought, break your journey for a few weeks back in Britain, then fly on to New York on the same flight from Heathrow that you always intended to use.

More relaxed flights

If you like going away for skiing weekends but don't want to pay for excess baggage, learn to fly or encourage a friend to learn – someone you trust! You can then hire a plane to share with several other people.

An alternative option is to contact a local flying school and ask if they have anyone going to a particular destination, who is willing to take you. Local airports can also tell you about smaller, reasonably cheap airlines, which give a more informal service, such as Scot Airways, 01223 292525, www.scotairways.co.uk, which flies from London City to Dundee and to Amsterdam from Cambridge.

Access to VIP airport lounges without paying for first class tickets

Priority Pass is an annual ticket to airport's executive lounges, with their free showers, drinks, phones, faxes and private meeting rooms. £69 annual subscription gives you access to 266 lounges, worldwide and you pay around £15 each time you enter. Many canny business people fly economy and use this as a good way to soften the edges of a trip, especially during delays. Call 020 8680 1338 for details.

Airport parking
This is cheaper if you pay in advance. Check www.traveldirectorynet.co.uk/airport_parking/euro.php/airport_parking.html or phone the airport.

Reduced rates on the QE2
Magic Eye Breaks offer big discounts on most holiday brochure prices, but also has subscription-only newsletters listing 'magic prices' which are not simply last-minute bargains. The £20 subscription price is taken off your first holiday booking. They offer 25% off holidays, and hundreds off QE2 cruises. 0161 927 4777.

• I look forward to the advent of easyCruises, an easyJet venture, which aims to offer hop-on hop-off breaks on floating hotels in the Mediterranean and West Indies at £29 per night

Protecting your holiday money
Travel insurance does not cover you against the collapse of your travel company. However, under EU rules, any company offering a travel package

must offer further protection through another scheme. Also, if your travel company is an ATOL member, 0207 379 7311, www.atol.org.uk and your airline goes bust, you will be repatriated or, if you have not yet travelled, given a refund within four weeks.

Be careful with ABTA members, 020 7307 1907, www.abta.com if you book with a tour operator who is an ABTA member, you will be reimbursed in the event of a problem; but if you book through a travel agent who is a member, and your holiday-provider is not, you will lose your money.

AITO, 020 8744 9280, www.aito.co.uk guarantees your money back if any member goes bust.

Independent trust funds
Some travel companies have these, which are not ideal. Pay at least £100 of your holiday with your credit card to give yourself the protection of the Consumer Credit Act and if you have a problem, complain to the credit card company.
TTA, www.traveltrust.co.uk 020 8876 4458.

Protecting yourself
If you are bumped off a flight, don't be fobbed off with travel vouchers as compensation but ask for Denied Board Compensation. The Air Transport Users Council will take up complaints if you

cannot get compensation. 020 7240 6061 (Monday to Thursday).

On the other hand, if you are not in a hurry, you could ask if they need any volunteers to be bumped. You will be put on the next flight, usually with a free flight voucher in thanks.

If you have an accident or become ill, take witnesses' contact details and photos of any evidence to support your claim for compensation. Talk to Holiday TravelWatch, 0121 747 8100, www.holidaytravelwatch.com, write to Condé Nast Traveller magazine, Vogue House, Hanover Square, London W1S 1JU, 020 7499 9080, or leading travel law solicitors Irwin Mitchell, 0800 313 233, www.imonline.co.uk or consult the Trading Standards Institute, www.tradingstandards.gov.uk 0870 872 9008.

Don't buy flashy luggage

Brightly-coloured bags are cheaper to buy in shops and will distinguish yours among a sea of black bags. Designer luggage can draw attention to itself at airports and hotels, where gangs of thieves meet the redeye flights and can walk away with your luggage.

Do not relax your vigilance over your bags even at the hotel: the check-in desk can be an opportunity for someone to steal your wallet while you are occupied with paperwork.

• **Keepsafe is a system to help you recover lost property anywhere in the world. You receive a tag, which you stick on your valuable item like a mobile phone. It tells finders to call a free number – the switchboard – which will reunite you with your property. You can also add a temporary contact number if you are abroad. 0870 60 500 60, www.keepsafe.co.uk**

Wear your new things

Don't pack them. If your luggage is lost, it won't have your new things inside it.

Free maps

Reserve these from your local library, which also loans language courses. You can also download maps and plot your journey from home, using sites like www.journeyplanner.com and www.rac.co.uk to help you.

Foreign currency exchange

– You will not get the best rate at the airport. Order from home, preferably online, for the best rates. Many places deliver your currency, free, the day after ordering, or you can pick it up at the airport or a local post office. Shop around or try Marks & Spencer who have bureaux de change in their larger stores;
the Post Office, www.postoffice.co.uk
Onlinefx, www.onlinefx.co.uk 020 7224 5799
and Travelex, www.travelex.co.uk 020 7421 2300.

– Don't take out more currency than you need
just because your money-changer offers
'commission-free buy-back'. Although you won't
pay commission, they will make money by
buying back at a lower rate than you paid them.

– Some 'commission-free' money-changing
places have such a poor exchange rate, that you
may be better off finding somewhere that you
have to pay commission.

– Commission is always charged on travellers
cheques. You may be better off taking cash –
which you can put in the hotel safe – and
drawing extra, if you need it, with a debit or
credit card. The bank machines abroad will offer
you English instructions, but your card issuer
may charge you a transaction fee (1.5% to 2%)
and a 'currency loading fee' of up to 2.75%.

Bartering on holiday
Swopping goods while on holiday can be more
satisfying for everyone concerned, and you can
forget about exchange rates. Show your goodies
before suggesting what you want in exchange. A
bottle of Johnny Walker whisky crosses all
language barriers and can be your easiest way
of, say, getting a room in a fully-booked hotel.

Marlboro cigarettes can be swopped for taxi
journeys. Show as many packs as you mean to

pay before getting into the car, but hand them over only after arrival. A plastic digital watch may secure a day's rickshaw or taxi in poor areas, but in sophisticated areas, you may have to give a better watch.

Consider the locals' lives. If it freezes in winter, they will jump at good warm clothes, hats and gloves. They will value torches and batteries if there are power cuts. Jeans and baseball hats are always a favourite.

Trains and coaches

For prices for comparison, consult www.travel-browsing.co.uk/rail-bookings.html, or the National Fares Manual at reference libraries. The National Rail Enquiry Number (0845 484 950, www.nationalrail.co.uk) is bound to give you the best advice and should know about any special offers. Lots of discount fares are around, but book on the first day that booking opens – months ahead of the journey day – or you might not get the price you want. Many tickets stipulate in advance which train you must take there and back.

Railcards for students, for those under 26 and for families are worth getting if you travel frequently or are going on long trips. Also check out local travelcards in your region. Ask about Railrovers – tickets giving you the freedom of an area or the country for a fixed price over a month.

National Express coaches and smaller coach lines are cheaper than trains and often travel into city centres, saving a bus or taxi journey after the train.

• Advantage 50 Coachcard gives up to 30% discount for the over-50s. National Express Coaches, 0870 580 8080, www.gobycoach.com

ENTERTAINMENT

The best way to save money is to stay at home, out of the way of temptation to spend money.

Libraries
At the library, you can read newspapers, magazines, and books, without paying for heating your home. You can surf the Internet on the computers there for free, though you may have to book ahead. There are videos, DVDs and tapes to hire, for cheaper prices and longer hire periods than in a video shop. If you need a book, you can order it for a small charge: determined book-ordering counteracts the trend for libraries to stock up with trivia and saves you the cost of constructing expensive bookshelves at home, to hold books you will never read again.

Private libraries which also act as clubs
These are often in beautiful and historic buildings all over Britain. For an annual subscription of between £15 and £150, they offer an idiosyncratic mix of clubby services and

wonderful book collections. Find one by sending an SAE for the list of members to the Association of Independent Libraries, c/o The Leeds Library, 18 Commercial Street, Leeds LS1 6AL, 01132 453071.

Manchester's Portico Library, for instance, has an excellent collection of books and offers a good two-course lunch at £8, bring your own wine. The London Library has over a million books and is strong on new fiction, history, biography and old periodicals. Lending periods are in months rather than weeks and there are no overdue fines. If you live 'in the country' you can take out fifteen volumes by post. The staff helpfully find books from other libraries too, saving the cost of telephoning round and collecting them yourself.

• **The London Library, 14 St James's Square, London SW1Y 4LG, 020 7766 4720, www.londonlibrary.co.uk**

Free music, films and games

The radio is free – even freer if you buy a solar-powered one. If buying a new radio, buy a digital one (like the Pure Evoke, from www.unbeatable.co.uk) which gives you access to various extra free channels.

If you have a computer, you can listen to and download, for free or very cheap, various styles of music, films, games and software to suit all tastes. These sites change, so use a search engine like Google or AskJeeves and asking for 'free music', for example.

• Try www.dotmusic.com www.peoplesound.com
www.audiosurge.com www.mp3speciality.com
www.musicnet.com www.wippit.com
www.easymusicdownload.com www.pressplay.com
www.kazaagold.com www.musiccity.com
www.mp3downloadcenter.com www.mp3.com
www.artistdirect.com and www.kazaa.co.uk for sophisticates

• For software, try www.download.com
www.freedownloadscenter.com www.webattack.com
www.softwareseeker.com www.completelyfreesoftware.com
www.freewarefiles.com www.freesoftwareadvice.com

• For games, try www.realonearcade.com www.kazaagold.com
www.gamesdomain.com www.freeality.com
www.gamedemo.com www.vertexlabs.com
www.pcgameworld.com www.christiancomputergames.net
www.educationfinanceandloan.com

For free anti-virus protection, highly recommended for anyone who banks online, try www.grisoft.com.

Free Internet access

In many ways, it pays to use computers at Internet cafes rather than have your own. If the machine goes wrong it is not your responsibility, plus the assistants are on hand should you need help, all for a small fee. However, if you want to play with a computer all day for nothing, enrol on a part-time course at a local state college. Even if you are studying Indian Head Massage and the course runs only on Wednesday afternoons, membership of a college gives you unlimited free use of the Internet, and also access to other resources, like excellent libraries.

Books on tape

Listen2Books offers up to 55% off the recommended prices of lots of audio books, free p&p, and the catalogue includes many '2 for 1' offers, www.listen2books.co.uk 0870 191 3415.

The Tape Exchange is a national swop shop for audio books and CDs. To join, buy a cassette at £9.99 or a CD for £12.99 from their list of over 400 choices. You can do this by mail, from Welcome Break motorway shops or various other sites, nationwide. You can keep your tape or CD for as long as you want, or forever. If you want to swop it, return it, undamaged in its original box, or send it in, pay £2.99 (plus £1 p&p for the mail order option) and choose a new one.

• **The Tape Exchange, Carlton Towers, Goole, Yorkshire DN14 9LZ, 01405 861951**

CD-ROMS and games for £2.99

The Entertainment Exchange is the Tape Exchange's sister business, a swop shop for CD-ROMS and computer games. Find your nearest Welcome Break service station and buy your first CD-ROM (from £4.50) or computer game (from £7.99). Use it as long as you like and, when you want to swop, take it (undamaged) to any Entertainment Exchange and swop it for another one for £2.99. Or you can simply keep the CD-ROM or game. See the Tape Exchange above for contact details.

Cheap DVDs and videos from America

Buy a video or DVD player which can play American tapes or DVDs and get a friend over there to send you the latest releases in America.

Rental DVDs

www.screenselect.co.uk will post you an unlimited number of films a month for £9.99 per month, p&p free. The Gold Plan allows you to take out three DVDs at any one time for £14.99 per month.

Second-hand DVDs and videos

Choices Direct sells pre-viewed videos or DVDs from £6.95. There is also a huge range of new DVDs, videos and audio book tapes, plus a

'bloodhound' service which, for a small fee, will
try to trace anything hard to find.

• 01733 232800, www.choicesdirect.co.uk

Cheap CDs And DVDs
Try www.101.cd.com www.cd-wow.com
www.moviem.co.uk   www.ukdvdplayers.com

Free digital TV
 o receive thirty Freeview TV channels, including
 Sky News and Cbeebies, interactive services and
 en digital radio channels including BBC Radio 4,
 ou can invest in an adapter for around £99 or
 uy an iDTV (integrated digital TV) from any TV
 tailer. 0870 880 9980,
 www.bbc.co.uk/digital/tv/freeview
 for more information.

Save money by viewing films online
If you have a broadband connection you can
register at www.netbroadcaster.com and play
classic old films directly onto your computer
(beware of the increase in advertising emails
though). Also try www.movieflix.com but
remember that downloading anything with
pictures in it, especially films, takes a long time: it
may be better to do it overnight.

Free TV heaven

Bradford's National Museum of Photography, Film and Television has five viewing booths seating four people each and a forty-seater viewing theatre which you can book, free, or just turn up on the offchance. Choose one or all of thousands of recordings of every top TV programme, then sit back and enjoy. Bradford, BD1 1NQ, 01274 202030, www.nmpft.org.uk and open 10am till 6pm except Mondays, but open bank holidays.

Saving money at the cinema

Cinema tickets cost less in cheaper areas of the country or town, even when the cinema belongs to a national chain. Mondays and Tuesdays tend to be low priced days; matinees are cheaper. OAPs can usually get tickets on some weekday mornings for £2. Some readers will recall Saturday Morning Pictures for children; this is now renamed Movie Mob and this children's film club costs £1.

- Odeon filmline for tickets, 0870 50 50 007, www.odeon.co.uk

Take your own refreshments rather than paying exorbitant sums at the cinema shop. Iced lolly moulds (product no 3509) cost £4.55 plus £2.95 p&p from Lakeland, 01539 488100, www.lakelandlimited.co.uk. Supermarkets sell microwave popcorn bags at around four bags for the price of one you buy in the cinema.

Free tickets to top shows

Ask your local stations for tickets to recordings of TV and radio programmes. The BBC has an organized system called Audience Services: call on the number below, Monday to Friday, 9am to 6pm, to either speak to someone or hear a recorded list of coming shows. For popular TV shows, try to book twelve weeks ahead, but you can get radio tickets a week beforehand, and if you're lucky, returned TV tickets on the day.

• **BBC Audience Services, 020 8576 1227. Save your phone bill by faxing a request: 020 8576 8802, or look on the Internet www.bbc.co.uk/whatson/tickets and email your request**

Free nightclub tickets

www.nightclubinuk.com offers these.

Free concerts

Many historic churches hold these at lunchtimes.

Half-price theatre tickets

You can buy half-price (plus VAT) good seats for top London shows on the day at The TKTS Booth, the brightly-coloured booth in Leicester Square. Don't be fooled by other ticket agencies which try to imitate this: the booth always has a queue.

Open from Monday to Saturday, 10am and 7pm
and on Sunday from 12pm till 3.30pm. You pay cash
only, plus a £2 booking fee. If you don't have time to
queue, it is also worth phoning individual theatres
and asking if they have any 'standby discount
tickets' on seats not sold.

• **For more information, try the Society of London Theatres, 020
7836 0971, www.officiallondontheatre.co.uk**

Free days out at National Trust houses

Each National Trust property has a free day each
year. Call the regional office of the attraction of
your choice and ask when it is.

• **The National Trust Information Line is 0870 458 4000,
www.nationaltrust.org.uk**

Free admission to over 200 galleries, museums and historic houses

The National Art Collections Fund is the largest
charity supporting our public art collections. An
annual subscription gives you free entries to lots
of lovely places to visit throughout Britain, like
Kensington Palace, and discounted entry to
special exhibitions at the Royal Academy,
National Galleries of Scotland and Tate galleries.
Membership costs from £28 for under 18s to £55
for a family – check which rate is right for you.

• **The National Art Collections Fund, Millais House,**
7 Cromwell Place, London SW7 2JN, 020 7225 4800,
www.artfund.org

Discounted new books

www.amazon.co.uk sells books at a discount
and acts as a marketplace for you to sell your
second-hand books.

Bibliophile Books sell publishers' remainders at
under half price plus £3 p&p by mail order from
a catalogue of three thousand books under all
sorts of headings. Unit 5, Thomas Road, London
E14 7BN, www.bibliophilebooks.com 020 7515
9222.

www.bol.com have the latest bestselling books
at up to 60% off.

CHILDREN

Having a baby can be a very expensive business. Cradles are a huge waste as they last only a few months, so consider buying second-hand ones, or adapt a drawer. The vital thing is to buy a new mattress with safety holes in it, so the baby can breathe. Also choose multi-purpose equipment, for example, a baby swing that becomes a rocking chair, or cots that become beds or sofas.

Nappies

You can do without scented nappy disposal bags: carrier bags serve the purpose just as well. Instead of expensive wet wipes, take a bottle of water and cotton wool.

Cheap disposables are a false economy as they often leak so that you have to change a child's clothes. Save money on disposables by using the newest terry nappies when possible (though you will still need disposables for travelling). They fasten with press studs rather than pins, and are easy to use and wash.

For a selection, try Nappyline, 01983 401959,
www.wen.org.uk/nappies or Waitrose.

Information lifeline
The National Childbirth Trust is an excellent
source of contacts, ideas, free teas, nannies, finds
and shares and equipment for sale and hire,
including breastfeeding pumps. You need only
local membership, not the more expensive
national membership.

• 0870 444 8707, www.nctpregnancyandbabycare.com

Best lavatories
When railway stations charge 20p for toilets,
check the Station Hotel next door, whose
washrooms are usually in the basement. Large
department stores are free, clean and
wonderfully well-equipped, sometimes with
complimentary nappies and wipes.

Free baby food and other goodies
When you have a baby, your Health Visitor will
give you all sorts of free samples and coupons,
after you have a baby. Ask her for the Bounty
Baby Book. Most manufacturers send free
samples if you get yourself onto enough
relevant mailing lists, like the Baby Clubs run by

Tesco, Huggies Club or Cow and Gate. Look on the Internet or get the helpline phone numbers from the packaging of whatever you are interested in. For instance, Milupa sends baby food, 0845 762 3628, www.milupa.co.uk to new parents.

Reciprocal babysitting

Join or start a babysitting circle in your area. Tokens are given per hour or half-hour that your children are 'sat' and received when you sit someone else's children. Also see my information about au pairs on page 139-40.

Entertaining toddlers for free, or very cheaply

Most local authorities run professionally supervised playgroups called 'one o'clock clubs'. Many open first thing in the morning, close for lunch then have a second afternoon session. They cost around 60p a time. Carers have to stay, but a few pence buys a cup of tea and a biscuit, and there are magazines to look through while they play. Check details with your council.

If you live in a 'Surestart' area – which gets extra Government money – and you register with Surestart via your local authority, playgroups like this may be free, together with free tickets for swimming baths and seaside outings.

Libraries usually offer storytelling once a week for tinies, free. Also use the library to check out your local churches and community associations for other playgroups. Also check local museums.

Most local authorities run toy libraries. Aimed primarily at childminders, anyone can use them, and they allow you to borrow toys free from the central collection. You can duplicate this idea among a circle of friends, especially swopping puzzles – as long as everyone is honourable about returning all the pieces.

Early Learning Centres 01793 831300, www.elc.co.uk have lots of demonstration toys to play with, usually on Tuesdays.

• *Entertaining and Educating your Preschool Child* by R.Gee and S. Meredith is recommended by my readers and costs £7.19 or £4 second-hand plus p&p from www.amazon.co.uk

Do something different
Plan a theme day. Watch planes at the airport, then give them an airline meal at home using old chilled food containers of different sizes on a tray. Make them do the safety routine before they can eat.

Another idea is to have snail races which are fun and free and the snails don't seem to mind as they don't know they are racing!

Baby equipment and toys

Tie balloons of all colours and sizes onto various lengths of cotton, and tie them onto a lightweight piece of dowelling suspended between two chairbacks or anywhere where the baby can safely lie. She or he will love watching them move with the air and eventually learn to kick them.

Plastic kitchen jugs and equipment make good, cheap bath toys.

• Nippers, www.nippers.co.uk is a chain of toy and equipment shops which keeps prices low by operating out of farms, where children can also enjoy the animals. Branches in Canterbury (01227 832006), Chessington, Surrey (020 8398 3114), Colchester (01787 228000), Milton Keynes (01908 504506), Norwich (01953 601901), Royston, Herts (01223 207071), Rugby (01926 633100), Taunton (0182 335 0005) and Worcester (01386 750888).

Tracking down replacement toys

If your child becomes fond of a particular soft toy or train, buy a second, spare one and hide it. Come the day when the toy gets lost or damaged, you can triumphantly produce the new one. Otherwise, try Arbon & Watts 0870 012 9090, www.mailorderexpress.com who operate a 'toy detective' service.

Water games
Leave a garden sprinkler running in the garden to entertain children of all ages. It is better value than a paddling pool, and will water the lawn at the same time.

Somerset House, The Strand, London WC2R 1LA, 020 7836 8686, has an amazing courtyard with a series of fountains built into the pavement, which spurt irregularly. Children of all ages will spend at least an hour dodging between the columns of water, or running around hoping to be caught in the water. Meanwhile take changes of clothes and a flask, or enjoy a cheap cup of tea at the waterfront cafe, one of the loveliest and cheapest views in London. To round off the day, take them to see the buskers at Covent Garden and the Theatre and Transport Museums across the road.

Tire them out for nothing
Children under 15 go free with an adult paying £5.50 (£4.50 for concessions) on a London Walk or day out in the country. There is a huge variety of guided walks, all day and all week, seven days a week, mornings, afternoons and evenings, and I recommend Jack the Ripper. It costs 50p less per walk if you buy a Discount Walkabout Card for £1.

• London Walks, 020 7624 3978, www.walks.com

Remember that most London museums are free now and those which are not often have deals such as free days once a week or month. Special exhibitions and events may cost an extra fee. Other attractions in London include Portobello Road, where Paddington Bear fans can follow in his footsteps and see antique stalls, and Coram's Fields in Bloomsbury, where adults can enter to admire Winnie, the fat pig, only when accompanied by a child.

• **For more ideas, try www.travelforkids.com**

Nature and history walks

Your local council will have details of free nature walks through the year, which should include interesting bat-spotting nights.

Cheap tickets to attractions

The London Pass, 01664 500107, www.londonpass.com costs from £12 a day, and gets you into sixty tourist haunts from the Tower of London to Windsor Castle and the Cutty Sark, and can be bought with or without transport.

A week in which children go free

Kids Week is usually the last week in August. During this week, there are lots of free tickets for children to see shows in London, with backstage tours, 'meet the stars' sessions and opportunities to learn the secrets of stage make-up or dance or stage-fights. There are also free children's meals at several trendy London restaurants and the chance to travel and stay free with Superbreak and Hilton Hotels.

• For more information, contact www.officiallondontheatre.co.uk
The Society of London Theatre, 020 7557 6700

Parties

Abbey National's recent research found that spending on a child's birthday averages £110 for gifts and £100 for a party, peaking at £140 for the 10 to 12 year old age group. (For a free copy of Abbey National's Easy Guide to Kids' Parties, on how to host the perfect party without breaking the bank, call 020 7419 7330.)

When it comes to reducing spending on children's parties, you can try Ruth Deans' suggestion: 'Avoid hall hire and entertainer costs by holding a football or sports party in the park. Take a picnic or get pizzas delivered. If you dare, use nappy bags as party bags – but not for food!'

Local scout, cub, beaver or brownie guide leaders know all the best group games. Ask them if they would very kindly entertain your children's party for an hour in exchange for a personal payment or a donation to funds.

Hire an inflatable toy. Hire shops like HSS and others from Yellow Pages offer inflatable assault courses and all sorts of things, with assistants to blow them up if needed. You can also buy your own fête and fair equipment. Fete and Fayre sells and rents out all sorts of machines like candyfloss makers, hoopla equipment, a coconut shy, balloons and bunting, aimed at schools and clubs but are available to anyone. 020 8647 2964, www.feteandfayre.co.uk.

Eating out with children
Most decent places have children's menus starting at around £2.95 for a two-course meal with drinks. For instance, Café Med is a small London-based chain offering healthy food at £5 for two courses with an eating adult. All addresses and telephone numbers are listed on www.4london.info/londonrestaurantsmediterran ean.htm.

TGI Friday, 0870 225 5844, www.tgifridays.co.uk offers free refill fizzy drinks and coffee (not cappuccino or expresso) at all restaurants except Heathrow.

Help with homework
www.channel4.com/learning/microsites/H/hom eworkhigh has a panel of 100 teachers to help with tricky questions for children aged 9 to 16.

See www.bbc.co.uk/bitesize for other student-operated sites selling and buying homework services.

• For instant expertise in any subject, also try: www.abuzz.com www.askme.com www.allexperts.com www.knowpost.com www.expertcentral.com www.keen.com www.exp.com www.keen.com and www.infomarkets.com

Cheaper school uniform

– Make friends with the mothers of older children at your child's school. You will be given cast-offs if you go about it the right way.

– Don't buy separate shorts for boys in summer. Just cut down long trousers.

– Recycle name tapes. They last for around fifteen years. When ordering name-tapes for more than one child, there is no need to pay for more than one packet. Write only your surname, or if you want to be more personal, the first child's Christian name first; then your surname; then the second child's Christian name third, for instance 'Jane Wright Stephen'. When sewing the tapes onto clothes, just turn under the part that does not apply, so one child's clothes will read 'Jane Wright' and the other, the more public-school-sounding 'Wright Stephen'.

PETS

You can obtain pedigree animals from any rescue service in exchange for a small donation. Alternatively, find the pet breeders' association for the animal you want – via the Internet, business phone directory, pet magazines or the RSPCA (0870 555 5999, www.rspca.org.uk).

Pet charities like Cat Rescue will normally give you a voucher towards the cost of neutering a stray of the breed they support. Many breeders' clubs will also re-home rescued strays, and fully pay vets' bills for older animals.

If you want a new pedigree animal, ask for a 'pet standard' rather than 'show standard' animal. They are just as handsome but much cheaper. Also sold cheaper are animals too old for breeding or with physical defects which can, in my view, often make them more lovable.

Insurance
It is worth taking this out. Treating a dog with diabetes, for example, can cost £1200. But compare policies carefully and ask several important questions:

– Are there limits on the total payout per year?
More Than, 0800 300 885, www.morethan.com
offers a more generous £6000 limit for each and
every accident and illness.

– Do they give discounts for more than one
animal? PetPlan does this, www.petplan.co.uk
0845 071 8000.

– Will the insurer continue paying for ongoing
treatment, over a year?

– Will the insurer stop insurance when the pet
reaches a certain age? And if you take on an older
pet, will the insurer begin cover?
Marks & Spencer, 01244 681681,
www.marksandspencer.com and Direct Line,
0845 246 8246, www.directline.com won't start
insuring a pet older than 8 years old but will
continue cover if you start earlier.

– Do you pay the vet and then wait for
reimbursement, or does the insurer pay direct?

– Finally, are there limits on the amount of
reward the insurer will offer? And do they
answer the phone? When I lost my pedigree cat
one Saturday lunchtime, I was infuriated that my
insurers did not work on Saturday afternoons or
Sundays and therefore could not authorize me to
offer a reward until Monday. Furthermore the
reward was initially capped at a paltry £50 – not

enough to persuade a cat thief to return a £200 cat.

Lost pets
Many people, including myself, invest huge sums
in microchipping pets, although this does not
always work in theft cases. A vet does not
automatically check an animal's number unless
asked to, and has no way of knowing if an animal
is stolen unless someone has found the animal and
queries its ownership.

However, there is a free pet search service,
0121 743 4133, www.ukpetsearch.freeuk.com
which uses 300 helplines nationwide.

COMPUTERS

I buy these from John Lewis, (020 7629 7711, www.johnlewis.com, 0845 604 9049 for a helpline as they are accountable and they have an aftersales service. You can also try the many electrical shops on Tottenham Court Road in central London for good, up-to-date technical equipment. Duty-free shops, especially abroad, offer brilliant bargains for techies, but it is difficult to return expensive goods if they go wrong.

If you are not looking for the most futuristic computer, the Morgan Computer Company can save you hundreds of pounds, with lots of computers priced at under £500, as well as all the accessories including digital cameras.

• **020 7255 2115 for the showroom or 01214 565565 for mail order, www.morgancomputers.co.uk**

Also check the clearance and end of line sections in the main computer manufacturers' websites.

Second-hand computers and spares
We urgently need special laws to govern the way that computers are sold. They are hellishly

expensive and you get no warning of extra expenses, such as the cost of inkjet cartridges for printers. However, Computer Exchange is a chain of shops selling refurbished computers and hard-to-get spares for so-called obsolete kit, in other words, over six months old. You can buy or swop items, the guarantee is said to be better than the manufacturer's and lasts a year, and you can phone the shop for technical help and information, or just pop in for a chat.

• Computer Exchange,0845 345 1664, www.2.cex.co.uk

Recycled toner and inkjet cartridges
Using recycled cartridges reduces printing costs by around 80% and reduces waste. Empty Cartridge will buy empty cartridges from you to recycle them – and will collect or you can freepost these. It also offers good multibuy deals.

• www.emptycartridge.co.uk, 01252 675727.
Also check www.inkcycle.co.uk/noflash/empties.html
www.hungryinkjet.com   www.mouse2housedirecto.com and
www.cartridge-fill.co.uk

Phones, camcorders and digital cameras
Try www.withandwithoutwires.co.uk, 0870 240 5522. When I looked, there were BT phones at £3.99.

STATIONERY AND POSTAGE

To re-use envelopes you don't need expensive sticky labels, simply strike out the address and write the new one elsewhere on the front.

Write on both sides of a piece of paper. For rough paper, beg boxes of mistakes from local printers or if you spot a business which is moving premises, offer to take their old headed paper off their hands.

Save on postage
– Send things by email or fax. Access to fax machines should not cost more than 5p per page at local businesses or at the library.

– Save stamps by knowing what to ask for at the Post Office. Don't send things by registered post, which is meant to insure valuables, when recorded delivery, next-day delivery, or even a free Proof of Postage certificate would do. Don't bother to send things by Special Delivery on Friday as the Post Office doesn't deliver on Saturdays. Try a minicab or a delivery firm instead if it is urgent.

– Registered and recorded delivery can actually slow an urgent package down by a day, since it has to be tracked. If you want to check the progress of your parcel, try www.royalmail.com or 0845 774 0740 or Parcelforce, www.parcelforce.com or 0800 224 466.

– Get money off parcels sent abroad. From Michael Honychurch comes this tip to save money on parcels weighing under 2kg sent abroad. Write 'small packet' on the outside. On the largest parcel, this saves nearly £3 on the regular fee. You can enclose personal correspondence such as a birthday card, but not reams of official papers. You may have to point out to the clerk at the Post Office that you are entitled to pay the cheaper rate.

– Nearly one in ten first-class letters arrives late. Homes and businesses will soon be able to claim up to £10 compensation for each letter delivered late, both first and second class. The rate is £5 if there is clear evidence of delay and £10 for longer than ten days' delay. If late delivery is hard to prove, you can claim twelve first-class stamps. The sender *or* the receiver (not both) can claim compensation and you should check on compensation available for special delivery and parcels if they are late. For more information see the Post Office leaflet 'We want to help you', or ring Royal Mail enquiries, 0845 774 0740

– If you are in a business bidding for a contract and your bid arrives too late, you can potentially lose a great deal of money. You can insure against this loss for a small fee – ask at the Post Office before sending your letter.

Cheaper stationery

Staples, 0800 141 414, www.staples.co.uk and Viking Direct, 0800 424 444, www.viking-direct.co.uk sell everything from reams of paper to office chairs at cheap prices for bulk, and with same or next-day delivery even on a box of paperclips. You often receive extra freebies with certain orders.

• **Office World has fifty-six national superstores and a mail-order catalogue offering a best-price guarantee. 0800 500 024, www.office-world.co.uk**

Free birthday cards

Hundreds of websites offer to send free e-cards. www.talkingbuddy.com (animated and talking cards); www.happybirthdaytoyou.com (singing cards); www.123greetings.com www.bluemountain.com automatically sends e-cards to everyone in your e-diary when appropriate. Or to make your own, download clip art free from www.freeimages.co.uk

Cheap greetings cards

Try Card Fair, whose prices start at 49p. 01462 492200, www.cardfair.co.uk

MR THRIFTY'S CHRISTMAS

If you are socializing with friends after Christmas, why waste time and money shopping before? You will be able to give them better presents by waiting for the post-Christmas sales.

• **Travel Paraphernalia is full of cheap, useful gifts for all ages, that cost under £5. In the current catalogue, I found a smart pack of slimline playing cards, £5.99 (item no G/3255); a survival whistle, £3.99 (item M/1998); an emergency mobile phone charger, £4.99 (M/3376) or a spectacle repair kit, £1.99 (M/355), p&p £3.99. PO Box 16, Banbury, Oxon OX17 1TF, 0870 120 3097, www.travelparaphernalia.com**

Don't give trophy presents
Don't beggar yourself to impress rich people. Millionaires are delighted with ordinary things they never see, like a book of stamps or this book. They also particularly like small toys.

Give small, beautifully wrapped presents
– A jar of marmalade from Fortnum and Mason is delicious. Or buy a jar from school or club Christmas fairs.

– A nail varnish from Chanel, for instance, costs only a few pounds but comes beautifully wrapped. 020 7493 3836, www.chanel.com. This suggestion is from Fiona Temple.

– A book like *Bizarre Books* by Russell Ash and Brian Lake, £6.99 plus £3.95 p&p, Hawkin's Bazaar, 01986 782536, www.hawkin.com for catalogue or shops.

– Offer your services in a coupon offering cooking, shopping, washing-up, car washing, handyperson services or babysitting.

– Homemade chocolates or cake are the best.

Send presents early
Second class post is cheaper. Or some suppliers will send items direct to the recipient, so you don't have to wrap and send it on.

Decorations
Marks & Spencer and Early Learning Centre sells homemade Christmas crackers, which you add your own presents. Hawkin's Bazaar, as above, sell these, as well as old-fashioned paper chains you stick together and hang around the room.

Also try to wangle a trip to a florist's wholesale supplier via your local florist. They have lots of decorations and accessories you don't normally see.

Christmas trees

For a cheap real tree, go to your local wholesale
fruit and vegetable market – Manchester is
considered the best Christmas tree centre in
Britain – or seek local nurseries (not garden
centres, too expensive). Non-drop needles are
best, because the others clog your vacuum
cleaner.

• **The British Christmas Tree Growers' Federation can give you
nearest supplier. www.christmastree.org.uk, or Roger Hay, 01314
470499 or 07831 418886**

Christmas cards

Cut out a simple stencil shape like a star, lay it on
the Christmas card and paint round it. For
eccentric art you can photocopy, try the Dover
Bookshop, 020 7836 2111, www.doverbooks.co.uk
– another excellent and cheap source of eccentric
presents, like the cut-out dolly book of American
presidents.

Wrapping paper

Plain brown paper purchased by the roll looks
good, tied with rough string or ends of wool.

Feasting

Keep your nerve. If you want a turkey, wait until
Christmas Eve when the prices really drop. Or
look at alternatives: chicken and beef are both

good value at this time of year. Smaller cuts of meat are good value, and don't need finishing up.

• **Club together with others to buy turkey and other meat from Hockeys Farm, where a £75 order is delivered free. This is a farm where animals are naturally and kindly reared. 01425 652542 for details, including other national distributors**

SAVING TIME, MONEY AND TEMPER – COMPLAINING

Get a refund, not a repair
Like people, machines have characters. If your new machine breaks down, refuse the shop's offer of a free repair. This is entering a circle of hell in which you have legally 'accepted' the machine and can't claim your money back when it goes wrong for the umpteenth time later. Instead, ask for an exchange or your money back (don't accept a credit note, unless there is nothing wrong with the machine and you have simply changed your mind about it).

A useful guide for shoppers
'No refund on sale goods' notices are illegal. This is one of the useful points in a booklet published by the Department of Fair Trading called Shopping with Confidence. This general guide to your consumer rights, and others dealing with specific problems like buying shoes, are available from 0870 606 0321, www.oft.gov.uk

Complaining

I would like to complain that it is usually necessary to complain before you get what you have paid for. Some weeks, I have saved more money by complaining than I have earned.

Big companies can run rings around the law, inventing often crazy excuses not to refund money. Many have adopted a rule that 'you can only claim a refund if you take it back within twenty-eight days' which does not stand up in law.

Some key points to remember when it comes to complaining include:

– Get the names of people you talk to when you are complaining, and keep a brief diary of who you spoke to, when, and what they said.

– Work out what you want as a result of your complaint. 'I want my money back/this product changed/someone to say sorry', etc.

– People say you shouldn't digress, but stick to your point. Personally I can't resist embroidering my complaint, making it as florid, personal and full of dark emotion, crisis and emergency as possible!

– Persist. Ask for the next person up in the chain of command as they will have more clout. If you are kept hanging on, use directory enquiries to find the ordinary business number of the business headquarters, rather than its 0800 number. Phone in and ask to speak to the Managing Director's secretary. They usually sort things out. I have used this technique professionally, when worn out by BT Press Office, whose way of sorting out my readers' problems and queries is simply not to reply to press queries.

– Don't swear. It can be used against you.

– If you find someone who can sort out your problem, get their direct line, thank them afterwards and purr, 'May I always phone you from now on? You seem to understand my needs.' They should be putty in your hands.

Getting legal advice

Avoid going to law if possible: getting justice is costly and difficult. Even the Small Claims Court, which now also operates on the Internet, cannot enforce its judgements if, say, you are claiming money back from someone, without costing you a lot more ultimately.

Trading Standards Officers (through your local council), the Citizens Advice Bureau and sometimes local authority Law Centres give free legal advice. Many solicitors offer half an hour's free advice, but I suspect this is in some cases a way of tempting you into getting more, and paying.

Most household insurance policies include a free legal advice phoneline to give you advice on thorny problems. Many unions or trade associations have a free lawyer: the smaller ones tend to be best. My union, the British Association of Journalists, is always there in the most personal way, will pay for specialist legal advice when needed and offers quite wide-ranging insurance.

• The Consumers Association has a legal advice service with a quarterly charge of £9.75 for members and £12.75 for non-members. If they take a case further and have to write a letter, rather than simply talking on the phone the cost rises. 0800 920 123 or 0800 252 100, www.which.net

• The Accident Line is a free service backed by the British Medical Association offering thirty minutes' free advice to accident victims about compensation from specialist solicitors. 0800 192939, www.accidentlinedirect.co.uk

No-win, no-fee solicitors advertize in newspapers and on TV. They take on a limited number of cases and those will be safe bets – and they will take a large percentage of your winnings.

• The Solicitor's Pro Bono Group may refer deserving cases to solicitors prepared to pursue them free. 020 7929 5601, www.probonogroup.org.uk

Saving money on solicitors

If you are paying a solicitor, don't treat them as a friend. Write down the facts, names and addresses before your meeting and never chat. If they ask how you are, say, 'Fine' even if you're on your last legs, as the timed meter is ticking and you may be charged for exchanging pleasantries! It's cheaper to write your own letters based on their advice. Add the magic words 'Without Prejudice' at the top, then your amateurish efforts cannot be held against you if the thing gravitates to court.

Solicitors are supposed to give you written costs for each job, but rarely do. If a solicitor overcharges, the following, kindly supplied by Vanessa Ward, may help:

'The agreement reached as to your agreed remuneration was not in writing purusant to Section 57(3) of the Solicitors Act 1974 and therefore the agreement is not enforceable against me.

I should like to draw your attention to Rule 15b (I) and (ii) of the Solicitors Practice Rules 1990 as revised in February 1991 by the Council of the Law Society (no. 13.08 of the Guide to the Professional Court of Solicitors, sixth edition, page 284). I did not receive from you either confirmation of my instructions in writing or a record of the agreed fee, as recommended. It is your duty to clarify any agreement as to the payment of your costs.'

If you are still not happy with their response, threaten to complain to the Office for the Supervision of Solicitors (01926 820082, www.oss.lawsociety.org.uk) who may 'tax' the bill, meaning look it over and make the solicitor cut it down. Solicitors hate this as it involves time and fuss, and they will probably make you an offer to go away.

• **The website www.chambersandpartners.com ranks solicitors and discusses their reputations if you read between the lines**

• **The Law Society's website www.solicitors-online.com (0870 606 6575) lists all solicitors in England and Wales by specialism; for Scotland, it is www.lawscot.org.uk (01312 267411, ask for the Records dept)**

• **For family affairs, members of the Solicitors' Family Law Association (www.sfla.org.uk, 01689 85 0227) are bound by a code of conduct to keep costs down and settle matters amicably**

Ombudsmen

Before spending money on a solicitor, find out if the company you are complaining about has a complaints scheme, or is a member of a trade group which may have an independent complaints procedure. These are not always 'independent' but can be biased towards their members who fund the service.

There may be an ombudsman. These are great final arbiters, to whom you may complain without having to go to court. Organizations aren't bound to accept their rulings but they usually do if the ombudsman has any teeth. But check first: some ombudsmen do not have jurisdiction over non-members of a particular industry. For ombudsmen not listed here, check Thomson Local Directories or Yellow Pages.

Also bear in mind a horror story concerning a man who received a £500 payout as a result of the Pensions Ombudsman's ruling. His opponents are appealing to the High Court – and he must foot the bill for his own defence.

• **Financial Ombudsman Service, 0845 080 1800, www.financial-ombudsman.org.uk includes complaints about personal pensions, insurance, investments, banks and building societies**

• **Pensions Ombudsman, 020 7834 9144, www.pensions-ombudsman.org.uk includes complaints about occupational pension schemes, trustees and administrators**

• **Ombudsman for Estate Agents, 01722 333306, www.oea.co.uk**

• **Office of Legal Services Ombudsman, 0161 839 7262, www.olso.org includes barristers, solicitors and conveyancers**

• **Adjudicator's Office, 020 7930 2292,
www.adjudicatorsoffice.gov.uk includes complaints about
the Inland Revenue, Valuation Office Agency and Customs &
Excise**

• **Independent Complaints Reviewer, 020 7278 6251,
www.icrev.demon.co.uk/icrbook.htm includes complaints
about the Land Registry, Public Record Office, Charity
Commission and Housing Corporation**

Misuse of power at local level is one of the
biggest wastes of time and money. If you feel
your Parish Council is acting poorly, or a
neighbour dispute is being pursued illicitly by
a person misusing their power, contact the
Standards Board via the Department of
Transport and Local Government. I have been
sent round the houses when trying to find one
definite number for this, but try 0845 078 8181
or 0800 107 2001, or www.standardsboard.co.uk.

There seems no legal way of checking a local
council who you think is frittering away your
money, unfortunately. For other cases of
financial abuse, you can try the National Audit
Office. I have found them less heroic than I
supposed, when trying to find out
information, but this is one of the last bastions
of defence against odd goings-on,
www.gsi.gov.nao.co.uk 020 7798 7000.

Journalists

Newspapers safeguard our proud tradition of free speech, and they can be your best line of defence against injustice, as long as you can find a journalist to listen to your story. The *Sunday Times* does excellent investigative work; sometimes so does the *News of the World*. Read the papers and write, phone or email the person named on an article similar to your needs or subject of complaint. Continue trying to contact them if even you initially have no luck: they honestly are snowed under, and your best strategy is to persist.

When complaining to a journalist, provide full details of your case, preferably in bullet points, with all your daytime and evening contact numbers and the names and numbers of anyone you dealt with.

• In cases of dodgy dealing with banks and building societies, check the superb 'Jessica Investigates' in the Saturday *Daily Telegraph*

AND FINALLY...

Discounts, fun and fighting for the rights of elderly people

ARP O50 is the Association of Retired People and offers members all sorts of discounts, including on travel and insurance. 020 8764 3344, www.arp050.org.uk for details.

Making a will

Steer clear of banks, building societies and lawyers, unless you have legal complications such as a farm changing hands. They will charge large fees and can take a long time.

Take out a free thirty-day trial of Which? Online, where there there is a new full will-writing report including advice on making bequests and appointing executors.
www.trial.which.co.uk/legaladvice, 0845 307 4000. You can also find information from www.rememberacharity.org.uk, 0808 180 2080. You are not allowed to make rude comments about others in your will and, although I am not a lawyer, I believe the best way to cut someone

out of your will is to leave them a small amount and say why: 'I bequeath so and so 1p because they have previously had money from me' should secure your will against being legally queried after your death.

I am not overly impressed by will-making services, which aim to make money in the long-term by charging you for storage. If you decline the offer of storage they can get unpleasant as they know this is a cheaper option. However, some will-making services offer cheap introductory rates. Check in the back of Saturday newspapers for the small adverts offering these.

Most big charities have Legacy Officers who will help you to make a will, free, if you leave money to their charity. If you suspect someone is likely to challenge your will after your death, professional willmaker Stewart Smith points out that it is a good idea to leave a charity some money. Then if your will is questioned, the charity will employ professionals to fight for itself, and incidentally, the other legatees.

Appoint two younger friends as executors. Keep your affairs in perfect order, with a master list of insurance policies, and what you owe and own, to hand. I have found officials tremendously kind and helpful in offering advice and hints about how to save money once you do your own probate.

Arranging a funeral

People don't shop around for a cheap funeral.
Like boasting that you bought an engagement
ring at a knockdown price, it is considered
indelicate. I considered it a duty to my late
mother, however, to find a good quality
undertaking service, without paying hundreds
more than I had to. She would have expected it –
which is more than the undertakers did. Many,
asked a straight question, could not supply even
the vaguest idea of their eventual bill.

Some local councils, for example, Wigan's, have
negotiated cut-price funerals for residents. Call
your local cemetery, listed in the phone book with
the council, and ask.

Planning ahead for your own funeral saves time
and money and gives you the opportunity to
specify your wishes. Rather than paying into a
funeral plan, it may be cheaper to put money
aside in a savings account, in the name of the
funeral organizer, otherwise the money will be
frozen on your death.

Cremation is cheaper than burial. It is also more
ecological and saves the upkeep of a grave. You can
be buried in your back garden, but it will reduce the
property value – though obscurely, 'larger
landowners' are advised to do this – I presume the
land is large, not the person. Get advice from the
Environment Agency, 0845 933 3111.

Better still are the new Woodland Burial Grounds, giving you the chance to return your body to Nature in beautiful surroundings for about half the cost of a conventional burial. You can find more details in the New Natural Death Handbook, £15.50, from the Natural Death Centre, www.naturaldeath.org.uk, 020 7359 8391.

People think they can save burial costs by donating their bodies for medical research, but few bodies are accepted – those which are whole, non-cancerous and within easy reach of a medical school. HM Inspector of Anatomy, 020 7972 4342, can give more advice, as can your local medical school.

If you are not religious, the British Humanist Association will send a trained representative to act as master or mistress of ceremonies, at prices comparable to churchmen. If you or a relative wants to conduct the service, ask for their booklet, *Funerals Without God* by Jane Wynne Willson with sample texts and poetry.

• £6.50 plus £1 p&p, 1 Gower St, London WC1E 6HD, www.humanism.org.uk

Or hire a good actor or toastmaster.